Praise for *Treatment Planning for Children with Autism Spectrum Disorders: An Individualized, Problem-Solving Approach*

"In the complex and challenging world of Autism Spectrum Disorders, this book offers a welcome, needed and thoroughly useful approach to planning treatment, whatever the setting, resources or problems. Chedd and Levine have managed to create a guide for educators, therapists and parents that is all at once practical and relevant, insightful and thought-provoking."

Richard Bromfield, Ph.D.
Harvard Medical School
Author, *Embracing Asperger's: A Primer for Parents and Professionals* and *Doing Therapy with Children and Adolescents with Asperger Syndrome*

"After introducing best practices for intervention in autism, Chedd and Levine present vivid case studies that bring alive the concept of matching methodologies and techniques to the widely diverse needs of individuals on the autism spectrum. My highest recommendation for anyone wishing to learn more about supporting those with autism."

Stephen M. Shore, Ed.D.
Assistant Professor of Special Education
Adelphi University
Co-author of *Autism for Dummies* and *Seven Keys to Unlock Autism: Making Miracles in the Classroom*

"Chedd and Levine make clear the foundations of Evidence Based Practice: vetting relevant research and using clinical judgment and experience to offer clients and families a range of options so that they can choose based on their own culture, values and individual needs in a true process of informed consent. In case examples Chedd and Levine demonstrate critical aspects of comprehensive assessment and the central organizing principle of ongoing reflective efforts to adjust the course of intervention. This book drives forward the effort to offer families rational choices and responsive intervention for children with Evidence Based Practices for Autism Spectrum Disorders."

Joshua D. Feder, M.D.
Director of Research, Interdisciplinary Council on Developmental and Learning Disorders
Graduate School

"Service providers and parents of children with ASD are often overwhelmed and greatly stressed by the explosion of "treatments" for autism, and the marketing and claims of effectiveness of specific approaches. Now that declarations such as 'Only *this* approach works for children with ASD' are no longer considered credible, there is an urgent need to support parents and professionals with a systematic process to guide individualized treatment planning based on evidence-based practice. Levine and Chedd have taken a huge step in meeting this need in this thought-provoking book that is both rooted in years of clinical experience and in-depth knowledge of the most current research, but exceptionally practical with intriguing case vignettes. A timely and much needed resource."

Barry M. Prizant, Ph.D., CCC-SLP
Director, Childhood Communication Services
Adjunct Professor
Center for the Study of Human Development
Brown University
Co-Author: of *"The SCERTS® Model"*

TREATMENT PLANNING FOR CHILDREN WITH AUTISM SPECTRUM DISORDERS

TREATMENT PLANNING FOR CHILDREN WITH AUTISM SPECTRUM DISORDERS

AN INDIVIDUALIZED, PROBLEM-SOLVING APPROACH

NAOMI CHEDD
KAREN LEVINE

WILEY

JOHN WILEY & SONS, INC.

Published by John Wiley & Sons, Inc., Hoboken, New Jersey.
Published simultaneously in Canada.

Library of Congress Cataloging-in-Publication Data:

Chedd, Naomi, 1952–
   Treatment planning for children with autism spectrum disorders : an individualized, problem-solving approach/Naomi Chedd, Karen Levine.
      p. cm.
   Includes bibliographical references and index.
   ISBN 978-0-470-88223-8 (pbk.); ISBN 978-1-118-25944-3 (ebk.);
   ISBN 978-1-118-23482-2 (ebk.); ISBN 978-1-118-22106-8 (ebk.)
   1. Autism in children–Treatment.   I. Levine, Karen, 1959- II. Title.

RJ506.A9C4424 2013
618.92'85882–dc23

                                                         2012017191

Printed in the United States of America

10   9   8   7   6   5   4   3   2   1

DEDICATION

For Graham, Harry, Kinsey, and Adam and in memory of my mother.

–N.C.

For David, Sue, Dan, Tim, Maureen, Seth, Kelsey, Brendon, and Rebekah.

–K. L.

TABLE OF CONTENTS

PREFACE

Treatment planning for children with autism spectrum disorders (ASD) requires educators and therapists to have a combination of big hearts filled with an appreciation for diverse and complex children, as well as keen and flexible minds that are able to make sense of confusing, sometimes conflicting, and ever-evolving clinical and research fields. How can this child be helped today with this problem or developmental challenge? This is the question those designing and implementing treatment plans need to answer. An approach to thinking about how to answer that question is what this book is about.

As clinicians and consultants to many families of children with autism spectrum disorders and other developmental disabilities and the schools and agencies that educate them, we have seen a broad range of interventions and combinations of interventions work in different ways for different children. Some work well for certain challenges for certain individuals at a specific point in their development, "fixing" or minimizing a problem and/or helping children learn and apply new skills, increase social interactions, form relationships, and enjoy activities that previously eluded

Michelle Aldridge, The University of Texas at Dallas; Susan Longtin, Brooklyn College; and Amy Laurent, University of Rhode Island and Emerson College. Special thanks to Josh Feder and Ruth Glynn-Owen for their encouraging and helpful comments reviewing early versions of Chapter 2 on Evidence-Based Practice.

We especially want to thank the children and families with whom we have the privilege of working, for sharing with us their challenges and triumphs, for being our best teachers, and for reminding us every day what is important.

ABOUT THE AUTHORS

Naomi Chedd, MA, LMHC, is a Licensed Mental Health Counselor specializing in working with children and adolescents with Autism Spectrum Disorders, Prader-Willi Syndrome, and other developmental disabilities and their families. She is a frequently invited speaker at local and national conferences. She also trains school-based professional and paraprofessional staff on effective practices for working with children with developmental disabilities and mental health problems.

Naomi has written numerous articles for popular and professional publications and is co-author with Karen Levine, PhD, of *Replays: Using Play to Enhance Emotional and Behavioral Development for Children with Autism Spectrum Disorders* (Jessica Kingsley, 2007). She lives in Brookline, Massachusetts, with her husband and three children.

Karen Levine, PhD, is an instructor at Harvard Medical School and a practicing psychologist in Lexington, Massachusetts. She was the co-founder and co-director of the autism program at Boston Children's Hospital in the 1990s and of the Autism Center at Cambridge Health Alliance. With Naomi Chedd, she authored *Replays: Using Play to Enhance Emotional and Behavioral Development for Children with Autism Spectrum Disorders* (Jessica Kingsley, 2007).

Karen has also authored numerous articles and book chapters. She served on the Massachusetts Governor's Autism Commission in 2011. She is the recipient of the 2010 Federation for Children with Special Needs Founders Award, and the 2000 Boston Institute for the Development of Infants and Parents Award for Excellence.

CHAPTER 1

INTRODUCTION: LOOKING AT TREATMENT PLANNING THROUGH A DIFFERENT LENS

Do any of these situations sound familiar? One of your students has just been diagnosed with an autism spectrum disorder (ASD). Should you change the way you're working with him? If so, how? And why? Or maybe a student has been in one of your autism programs for a few months or even a few years, and despite his having made gains in certain areas, you have an increasingly uneasy feeling that many of his challenges are not being addressed at all. Or you feel that a patient had made considerable progress in one type of school and home program, but his progress is slowing down. Or he is only making gains in one area, and you believe he could progress more rapidly with a different kind of approach, at this new point in his development and learning, which is different from his earlier learning profile.

Like most of your colleagues, you read books and scan websites, go to occasional lectures and workshops, and peruse articles about treatments for autism and about the importance of using evidence-based practices, and you want to know that you are, at least, understanding and implementing proven practices. But what does that really mean for you, working with your student or client tomorrow? Does hearing about others' successes and reading about certain studies guarantee that they will be useful in solving your specific student's problems? If an intervention has been effective with a large percentage of students according to one or even many studies, can you be sure that your student or patient will benefit from it? Or will your student fall into the category of children who demonstrated no significant change? Will you have overlooked a smaller study describing an approach designed for students more closely related to your student with a similar problem? Would it yield a better outcome for your student?

Defining Best Practices

Part of effective work with children involves continual monitoring and questioning what you are doing, wondering if you are taking the best instructional or therapeutic approach for your students, examining and reexamining your decisions about implementing available and emerging treatments, and considering and selecting certain interventions. Professionals in every discipline are bombarded with endless information on treatments for autism, and opinions vary as much as the treatments. One expert swears by one approach, whereas another is equally zealous but has the opposite opinion. Although research supports various approaches, professionals from different disciplines may interpret research results in entirely different ways. So the practicing professional—in an early intervention program, school, clinic, or other therapeutic setting, not to mention parents, who are eager to do the right thing for their child and want to get started as soon as possible—may be more confused than ever.

It is our premise that certitude regarding what is "the best treatment for children with autism" is a fallacy and can lead to ineffective and even harmful practice, while a cycle of continual questioning, planning, treating, monitoring, and revising informed by research as well as clinical expertise, leads to productive evolution in one's work with children.

Media Overload

It is almost impossible to flip through your morning newspaper, turn on the radio, or glance at a magazine in a grocery store checkout line without spotting something about autism. Although they offer a wealth of useful information and solid research, the popular media and especially the Internet also add to the confusion. Possible causes, personal accounts from celebrity parents, new brain imaging studies, and research findings on genetic links are only a few of the topics that may pop up on any given day. Of course, effective treatment (and some may dare to whisper the word "cure") is really what's on every practitioner's and parent's mind.

What should professionals do to provide the best help they can for their students or clients with an ASD diagnosis? What are the most important areas to work on? And in what order? What about the child who is too anxious to enter the classroom or office without melting down or the child who does the opposite of whatever you ask her to do? The child who bangs his head on the table in response to any demand? The child who seems to want to communicate but only makes an open vowel sound or screeches loudly when asked a question? The child who clearly wants to have friends but is so socially awkward that the other children avoid him? The preschooler whose parents have told you they want him "mainstreamed by first grade"? What treatments are going to help solve those problems or achieve those goals? Who should deliver them? Where? How? And for how many hours per week? And perhaps most important, what is the likely outcome? How do you know if you are doing the right thing? If you are helping?

Misinformation and misperceptions are rampant—about every treatment approach—and even about what autism is or isn't. But while opinions vary on all of these topics, virtually all professionals agree on one issue: Children with a diagnosis of autism should be educated and treated by providers with specialized training and experience with children with ASDs. The number of hours of treatment, the approach or combination of approaches, the level of structure it should have and in what manner, and how to define and measure success, continue to be debated. No single answer will solve all of the problems of the child with whom you are working.

A New Way of Thinking About Autism Treatment

In *Treatment Planning for Children with Autism Spectrum Disorders*, we are not advocating for or rejecting a specific technique or intensive intervention program. And we are not describing a new treatment that we think will "fix" autism. Rather, we propose a way of thinking about specific challenges and goals for individual children at a given point in their development that is structured around our interpretation of the most evolved current model of evidence-based practices. Currently, many treatment programs for children with ASD are "top down," starting with the treatment approach the provider or program believes is best supported for children with ASD, and then fitting all children with that diagnosis, which includes children with an enormous range of profiles, strengths, and challenges, into that model. We think of this as a "Here's the solution. What's the problem?" approach.

We instead emphasize starting with identifying the key questions one is planning to address, within the context of specific children at a particular time in their development, with their combination of challenges and strengths, their treatment history, and considering what has or hasn't worked in the past. We then recommend considering best practices based on a review of relevant research on treatments for the specific problem, challenge, or goal, with subjects like the child with whom the practitioner is working. Key variables such as age, general level of ability, other individual characteristics, co-morbid diagnoses, and type of family and school situation also need to be considered, as well as family preferences. Based on all of this information, the provider develops a treatment plan to address a specific problem and work toward a specific goal. The provider then evaluates the effectiveness of this treatment for this child over time, revising the plan if and when it ceases to be effective, the goals change, or the child changes.

Core Deficits of Autism

A diagnosis of autism is based on challenges across the domains of communication, social interaction, behavior, and play, according to the *DSM-IV-R* criteria (American Psychiatric Association, 2000). Challenges in each of these domains can range from mild to severe. Severity in one domain, such as communication, may not necessarily correlate with severity in any another, such as repetitive behaviors. Furthermore, children with an ASD diagnosis vary in IQ, from severe intellectual disability to intelligence in the superior range or extensive knowledge and competence in one particular area or subject, such as math or physics, or the ability to identify specific patterns. So devising a treatment plan to ameliorate the constant wandering or bolting of a nonverbal 3-year-old from storytime will be vastly different from a plan to support a talkative 8-year-old with Asperger's syndrome and far above-average intelligence, who is frequently running out of his classroom yelling "Everybody hates me!" Of course, it would be easier to apply one approach and set of strategies to every problem, but that wouldn't be sensible or responsible.

How the Book Is Organized

In Chapter 2 we discuss in some detail the subject of evidence-based practices (EBP), a subject that is on the minds of parents and professionals working directly with children, as well as the agencies that are making decisions about which treatments to fund.

Why There Is Confusion About EBP in Treating ASD

Evidence-based practice means using treatments that are supported by evidence indicating they are likely to be effective for the child with whom you are working, and for the goals on which you are working. This seemingly simple concept turns out to be remarkably complicated, often with no single clear path, and is especially complex in the autism treatment field. The complexities stem from several issues, some specific to autism treatment and some more generally present in education and therapeutic treatment. These include disagreement about what constitutes evidence and about which problems should be treated, as well as which outcomes one should measure. Additionally, because children with autism are so varied, treatments established as successful for one group may have little applicability for another child with autism but with a very different profile. Many studies of different treatments have been found to produce effective change, and there is no agreed-upon path to determine which bodies of research one should consider.

The context of treatment, including where a treatment is provided and who provides it, may also affect success. Different providers, parents, and agencies have differing philosophies and beliefs about autism and treatment, which certainly influences which treatments they are likely to choose for their child or themselves. How this should be weighed is also controversial. We will discuss in more detail these and other challenges to treatment selection, including contemporary conceptualizations of EBP. It is important to note that EBP in autism treatment is a very complex and dynamic topic, one that has been discussed and written about in great detail (e.g., Reichbow, et al, 2011). Our purpose is to put forth a practical model for treatment planning for those working directly with children, incorporating current principles of EBP, and not to provide an exhaustive review or discussion of this topic.

We will discuss some guidelines for thinking about EBP in the context of your particular situation, such as whether you are working with a child at home or at school, in a large group, small group, or one-on-one situation, and perhaps most important, what may be possible within the parameters of those circumstances. We will talk about a variety of treatment approaches, their developmental appropriateness, the usefulness and limitations of large-group research studies that look at treatment efficacy, and why children with the same diagnosis "on paper" vary in their presentations, not just in severity but also in their particular symptoms. For example, although one child may be extremely loud, active, and aggressive, another may be socially remote, silent, and underaroused. Yet both have an ASD diagnosis, display atypical behaviors, and are labeled, appropriately, as emotionally dysregulated. Treatment is more likely to be successful if one first identifies the problems and challenges that need intervention and then designs a treatment plan using one or several techniques, rather than assuming that one set of rules will solve all problems.

We will go on, in this chapter and in the case studies that follow, to describe why particular symptoms may be problematic in one situation and merit intervention but may not in another. One must determine under what circumstances and for whom the problem is a problem. Consider a 4-year-old who is beginning to get language, who may repeat the same words and phrases over and over, and understandably, may become annoying or disruptive in her preschool classroom, but her parents may be thrilled with her acquisition of language and not only tolerate it but encourage her constant chatter at home. Another 4-year-old, having recently mastered toilet training at school, has received a great deal of praise, naturally, but she constantly pulls her parents into the bathroom at home, sometimes several times an hour and during family meals, when dressing and undressing, at malls and at restaurants, thus delaying every family activity and creating chaos. In both of these situations, a behavior may be problematic in one setting but not in another, so a plan has to be designed that is flexible enough to address and shape the same behaviors in different settings.

In Chapter 3 we describe our treatment planning process. Although there are many ways to design and implement a plan, we think this is a sensible and flexible process that can be understood and implemented by parents and providers in various disciplines.

Case Studies

In the nine chapters that follow, we present case studies and describe different scenarios involving preschool-aged children through adolescents who have a diagnosis of an autism spectrum disorder, including Autistic Disorder, Pervasive Developmental Disorder, Not Otherwise Specified (PDD-NOS), and Asperger Syndrome. We have not included cases involving children with Rett's Syndrome or Childhood Disintegrative Disorder, both categories within the ASD spectrum. However, we have worked with children in both of these categories, and many of the techniques we describe are certainly appropriate for these populations as well. Each of the case chapters:

- Describes the scenario
- Identifies specific issues that are problematic at school, during after-school activities, at home, and/or in the community
- Identifies and prioritizes goals
- Outlines a process for creating a treatment plan
- Discusses ways to determine if the plan is successful—and what to do if one or more aspects of the plan are not

Approaches and methodologies referred to throughout these case studies include, but are not limited to, the following:

Applied Behavior Analysis (ABA)
Cognitive Behavioral Therapy (CBT)
Collaborative Problem Solving (CPS)
DIR®/Floortime™
Pivotal Response Training (PRT)
SCERTS™ Model
Early Start Denver Model (ESDM)
Positive Behavioral Supports
Relationship Development Intervention (RDI)
Sensory Integration/Sensory Diets

Social Stories™
Replays®
PECS

In each case study we integrate discussions of approaches and strategies, how they are similar and different, and how they can or can't work together. One intervention may be better at targeting a particular problem in a particular child in a particular situation, although two or three other approaches have a research base indicating that they are effective for treating the same problem. Rather than simply describing approaches in a decontextualized fashion, listing the pros and cons of each and reviewing available research, we discuss these approaches within the context of a case study, describing thought processes regarding the whys and hows of implementing one or more interventions. The differing perspectives of all the stakeholders and the interplay of those perspectives are major factors in most of these cases. There are times when one or more treaters, parents, or team members might change direction, redefine the problem, or have to focus on another, more urgent problem that surfaces during treatment. The goal throughout is to help readers design a developmentally appropriate, achievable treatment plan and answer the following questions:

- What are the most important problems to address?
- How does one set realistic long- and short-term goals?
- What does the child need to learn and accomplish—in the next two weeks, two months, or even two years?
- How can one create a treatment program that is most likely to work for an individual child?
- How does one implement this plan at school and/or at home—or in other settings?
- How does one determine if the plan is effective? How does one define and measure success?

Many more questions can and should be addressed, but these are often the major questions professionals and parents think about, no matter what the specific circumstances, whether the child is 3 or 13 years old, in a public or private school program, living at home, or in a different residential setting.

Along with the growing number of children identified with ASDs—1 in 88 according to a recent report from the Centers for Disease Control and Prevention (2008)—there is an increasing need and demand for ways to identify treatment approaches and programs that are likely to succeed. Professionals in the field and family members—psychologists, specialty service providers, school counselors, occupational therapists and speech and language pathologists, teachers and parents—need to make recommendations and decisions about treatments. How does one go about doing that? This is the main question we want to help you answer.

About the Appendices

We assume our readers have some familiarity with at least some of the approaches referred to in the case studies. We have included brief descriptions of these approaches in Appendix A.

In the following chapter, we discuss the concept of evidence-based practices within the context of treating children with autism spectrum disorders. We have tried to make this discussion of material that can fall, well, somewhere between "somewhat dry" and "dreadfully dull" relevant and practical. It may even prove to be thought provoking.

CHAPTER 2

WHAT IS EVIDENCE-BASED PRACTICE?

A Google-Scholar search of the term "evidence-based practice" in April 2012 yields an impressive 537,000 academic/professional articles or books related to this topic published in the past 10 years. When "autism" is added into the search term in conjunction with EBP, the number plummets to a mere 24,600. There is no doubt that this is an important topic! If one instead uses the general Google database to search "autism and evidence-based practice," so that agencies and other providers with websites or Internet listings are also included, in addition to articles and books, the number increases to 2,380,000.

One reason for these astounding numbers is that this topic is a major concern not only for researchers and authors but also for organizations treating children with autism, who, from varying philosophies, provide very different services, as well as for the agencies providing insurance coverage or reimbursement for these services. Virtually all of those agencies working directly with children with autism now claim to use evidence-based practices. How one defines "evidence" and how it applies to specific treatments and, most important, to treating specific children for specific challenges, are topics of much discussion and debate.

What Is So Important About EBP ?

The idea behind EBP is simple and logical: People who treat individuals should use methods that work, methods that have some established validity, to solve real problems. They should not, for example, arbitrarily decide to treat a 3-year-old's aggressive behavior in preschool by enrolling her in Spanish lessons. True, one could stretch and imagine a scenario where Spanish lessons could be a useful treatment for a 3-year-old's aggression: An American family who just moved to Spain has sent their child with autism, who had just begun to develop receptive and expressive English, to a Spanish-speaking preschool, and the child, suddenly unable to understand or to be understood, resorts to hitting when her English requests are not met with the expected response. This seemingly bizarre treatment choice highlights the importance of considering all the unique characteristics of each child, including context and clear understanding of the problem, when determining what treatment is likely to work and is most consistent with EBP.

Common Errors in Evaluating Treatments

Evidence-based practice, or using a sound process for treatment selection, prevents clinicians and educators from making several common human errors in perception that can lead to erroneous treatment choices. In some branches of medicine, problems are specific and homogeneous; research results are consistent; doctors agree on treatment; patients generally find the treatment acceptable and seek it out; and insurance providers, doctors, and patients agree on what should be covered. For instance, strep throat can be treated effectively in most patients with specific antibiotics. Because of the clarity of the problem (a simple throat culture can definitively establish this diagnosis) and the consistency in treatment success for a single category of treatment (antibiotics), it is straightforward for doctors and patients to work together to treat the problem, and funders agree to pay for this treatment. Although people of some religions and cultures do seek alternative treatments, in Western culture this is generally an accepted intervention based on consistent research outcomes, which are confirmed repeatedly by doctor and patient clinical experience. This treatment is so routine that, in most cases, neither doctor nor patient gives much reflective thought to the process.

In the autism field, however, this process is rarely as simple. Challenges can be enormous, yet treatments are rarely clear-cut or agreed upon. There are, however, great risks to selecting a treatment that sounds good with no treatment selection process. In the following sections, we briefly discuss common human errors guiding treatment in the autism field and other similarly complex fields. A process for selecting treatment based on some established evidence is formulated to avoid these errors, which are intrinsic to human nature. We humans, in the face of illnesses or disabilities that have great impact, without clear treatments that lead to cures, are particularly vulnerable to these sorts of errors in human logic.

Correlation Versus Causality

One common logic error that humans (and other animals) tend to make is interpreting correlation as causality. So, for example, if an individual listened to a certain piece of music before taking an exam of great consequence or competing in an athletic event and performed far better than usual, he might believe, at some level, that the song helped boost his performance. Then he might make it a tradition (superstition) to listen to that song before any similar event, even though the song probably had no impact on his performance. Just think about all the ballplayers who refuse to cut their beards or wear the same socks day after day during a pennant race, or the anxious fans who refrain from talking about a potential no-hitter, believing that somehow that might influence the outcome!

Similarly, many clinicians have had patients bring their child for one visit, and soon after, the child makes a developmental leap, such as starting to talk or make eye contact. Searching for some explanation and having positive feelings about the visit, the parents may falsely attribute the greatly anticipated and celebrated progress to something specific the clinician did, which is highly unlikely. However, simply relying on correlation and misinterpreting this as cause in planning treatment is unlikely to lead to the desired outcome and may even delay effective treatment or worse, cause harm.

Determining Treatment Effect When the Child Is Receiving Multiple Treatments

Another error in logic occurs when a child is receiving many treatments simultaneously and is making progress. It may be difficult, even impossible, to determine which treatment is the one helping the child or if the child is spontaneously improving. However, it is likely that both the child's family and the various treaters (e.g., the ABA therapist, special education teacher, occupational therapist) all have their own strong and possibly differing opinions about what is responsible for the child's improvement. Some treatments may not be helping at all or even impeding progress, whereas others may be making the primary contribution. Or perhaps the success is resulting from the particular combination of treatments, or the child is learning from experiences unrelated to any of the treatments.

Emotions Versus Logic

An additional threat to clear thinking and reasoning in the field of autism treatment planning is the power of parental love in the context of a treatment field with no clear or single path to progress. Many parents would do virtually anything if they thought it would make a significant difference in their child's success. Hence, the resulting vulnerability of parents can lead to the pursuit of treatment with claims and even testimony from other parents that this approach will "fix" their child.

Professionals, too, driven to serve their patients, may also be vulnerable to learning or developing treatments they believe are effective out of the same desire to help, in a field without one set of instructions and with children who may make very slow progress. Furthermore, people driven by desire for fame and fortune may take advantage of this vulnerability and, intentionally or not, promote erroneous treatments with claims of great impact. This potential vulnerability of those receiving treatment and potential opportunism in those providing treatment exist across many medical and mental health diagnoses where there is substantial impact but no clear cure or treatment path. For example, when the second author's (Levine's) late husband's cancer was running out of evidence-based treatments, their family was bombarded by well-meaning friends with articles about treatments with no support, that made no logical sense, and they too experienced this vulnerability. She remembers the rush of excitement and relief they both felt, as they—a psychologist and a physician—looked at a website that promised a cure for any incurable cancer, filled with optimistic, enticing before-and-after testimonials and photographs of people just like them. This is a crazy claim and suggests treatments not worth pursuing, which they realized one phone call later when logic returned. However, we humans, even scientists, are susceptible to dismissing logic, at least for a time, in the face of intense emotions. That treatments such as facilitated communication (FC) or administering the hormone secretin could gain as much support as they did for as long as they did is likely because of these factors (Mostert & Kavale, 2001; Sturmey, 2005).

Face Validity

Some treatments sound logical, especially to those without a background in the field, but have no actual support or basis. A company may claim they are able to "re-wire your child's brain by stimulating the social areas," with an illustration of exactly where autism occurs in the brain and an explanation of how this area would be stimulated with electrodes. This sounds sort of like doing physical therapy to strengthen weak muscles or even jogging to get in shape. However, knowing more about the brain and its complexities makes one realize this makes about as much sense as teaching your child Chinese by surrounding her with books in Chinese.

Like any other complex and constantly changing and evolving disease or disorder, the autism treatment field is filled with claims of quick cures if only parents would do this or that. New cures pop up that sound good, just as rapidly as old ones die out when it turns out they weren't effective after all, leaving thousands of disappointed, confused, and perhaps cynical but still hopeful families and providers in their wake.

How Can Treatments Be Evaluated?

Creating some system of checks and balances, accountability guidelines, or some way of determining that a treatment is a reasonable choice is important, so individual and societal time and resources are spent on studying and using treatments that have some likelihood of being effective. Establishing EBP guidelines sounds like a relatively simple procedure. Treatments, in order to be considered legitimate, should have to have some kind of proven track record or other evidence suggesting they are likely to work.

The complexity comes when operationalizing how one decides what "works" means, for whom, for what problem, for how long, and based on what sort(s) of evidence. On what basis does one determine, before beginning to treat an individual, which treatment is most likely to work?

If one consults evidence based on prior research findings, which research should be considered? There are excellent guidelines for determining research rigor, but even the most rigorous set of research studies that finds a treatment effective may not have relevance to whether the particular treatment will help the particular child and problem one is treating. Many other factors are likely to affect outcome, including (a) if the child has a very different profile, even within the autism spectrum, from the children studied; (b) if one is treating a problem not included in the problems studied; (c) if the context is different from that in the study; or (d) if the child or family finds the treatment objectionable.

History of Evidence-Based Practice in Psychology

Some background about the evolution of EBP is helpful in understanding some of the current controversies about its definition. The scientific method has been a part of applied psychology since the late 1800s (McReynolds, 1997), but the use of the term *evidence-based* (medicine) began in the medical field. By the early 1970s, it was specifically defined and quickly became accepted as meaning "randomized controlled trials validating effectiveness of a specific treatment" (Cochrane, 1972). Widespread use of the belief in the importance of this process spread quickly to many fields of practice, including psychology, speech and language pathology, and psychiatry. In the 1990s, psychologists and other specialists providing therapy (e.g., psychiatrists, social workers, behavior specialists) were under pressure to support the positive effect of therapies, especially with the quickly spreading use of less expensive psychotropic medicine options and increasing oversight of the health insurance industry and especially managed care. The APA set up a Task Force to develop criteria for designating a treatment as "well-established" or "probably efficacious" (APA, Society of Clinical Psychology, 1995, p. 10). Stringent criteria mirroring those from medicine were established. A list of treatments qualifying as "well established" or "probably efficacious" was then published (Society of Clinical Psychology,

1995). Factors such as clinical judgment, cultural fit, or patient or family preference were not incorporated into this early definition.

Brief History of EBP as it Pertains to Autism

There were initial attempts to establish EBP for children with autism through meta-analyses of research studies using the earlier, narrower iteration of EBP by the APA, the Division 12 stringent criteria (Society of Clinical Psychology, 1995, p. 10). Noted autism researcher Sally Rogers conducted the first such large-scale study and found that no treatment met these criteria (Rogers, 1998).

A special council was established by the Department of Education's Office of Special Programs to study this issue as it pertained to autism. Based on this committee's review, no specific treatment package was identified as being most effective. They concluded that

> although there is evidence that many interventions lead to improvements and that some children shift in specific diagnosis along the autism spectrum during the preschool years, there does not appear to be a simple relationship between any particular intervention and "recovery" from autistic spectrum disorders. Thus, while substantial evidence exists that treatments can reach short-term specific goals in many areas, gaps remain in addressing larger questions of the relationships between particular techniques, child characteristics, and outcomes. (National Research Council Committee on Educational Interventions for Children with Autism, 2001)

Several components of interventions likely to contribute to efficacy were identified, including entry into intervention programs as soon as an autism spectrum diagnosis is seriously considered, treatment of at least 25 hours per week, inclusion of a family component, low student-to-teacher ratios, sufficient amounts of adult attention in one-to-one and very small group instruction to meet individualized goals, a method for evaluating progress, and several other components (NRC, 2001). The committee's recommendations for effective treatment were based on empirical findings, information from selected representative programs, and findings in the general education and developmental literature. Interestingly, the NRC recommendations are quite consistent with the newer, broader definitions of EBP.

More recently, The National Professional Development Center on Autism Spectrum Disorders (ASD), funded by the U.S. Department of Education, Office of Special Education Programs, is a multi-university program that began on July 1, 2007 and continues to grow. The Center's mission is "to provide resources, professional development, and technical assistance that will increase the number of highly qualified personnel serving children and youth with ASD." This exciting, dynamic project continues to evolve, adding updated research reviews and training modules. Hence, providers who want to use and evaluate the effects of a specific technique can more readily access information and training about an increasing range of techniques that have research backing.

Since 2001, several more meta-analyses of the autism treatment literature have been published. Rogers and Vismara updated Rogers' 1998 review (Rogers & Vismara, 2008), and they found that still only the Lovaas studies met the EBP criteria in terms of raising IQ points but not definitively in other areas of functioning. Pivotal Response Training met the criteria for "probably efficacious" (Rogers & Vismara, 2008). Some meta-analyses have been conducted by groups or agencies promoting a specific philosophy (e.g., Wilczynski et al. ([The National Standards Project], 2009), which does not rule out validity but raises questions about objectivity or diversity in each of the many subjective issues discussed in this chapter that impact how a study's bearing on defining EBP is viewed. Each of the reviews has used different criteria for inclusion of research and has come to differing conclusions.

Some meta-analyses conducted over the past 10 years have examined studies of treatments for specific challenges in specific populations (e.g., anxiety in children with Asperger's, increasing joint attention in preschoolers), whereas others looked at whole-package treatment interventions. The more targeted studies for specific problems in specific populations can more readily be evaluated as applicable to the child with whom one is working. However, studying whole-package treatments is also important for multiple practical purposes, such as the usefulness of an agency or school program becoming expert in one specific model, or a parent choosing services when presented with two agencies using two different approaches. Odum et al., (2010) conducted a meta analysis using a complementary approach to prior meta analyses, rating comprehensive treatment models across multiple independent dimensions (e.g., Operationalization, Fidelity). In this way, one can readily spot potential strengths and weaknesses within models and determine if that particular strength or weakness is relevant to use of the treatment by a particular provider or program or for a particular patient or student. If a treatment is rated as low in "fidelity," for example, yet a service provider has advanced training and certification in the approach, this problem has minimal negative impact if the approach is deemed the best match for the child and problem in question.

Evolution and Expansion of EBP

A combination of the stringent nature of the early EBP criteria and the omission of softer clinical components crossing treatment methodologies that research had found and therapists across disciplines often clinically believed were important (e.g., therapeutic alliance, cultural sensitivity) led to the formation of a new APA Task Force in 2006. Its mission was to develop a new definition of Evidence-Based Practice in Psychology (EBPP) to address these criticisms.

The eventual result took into consideration clinical judgment and multiple patient characteristics when determining best practices. Hence, the concept of EBP within psychology has been greatly expanded since its original formulation. Not only does it encompass treatment informed by research, but it also includes clinical expertise with elaboration of the following components:

- Assessment, diagnostic judgment, systematic case formulation, and treatment planning
- Clinical decision making, treatment implementation, and monitoring of patient progress
- Interpersonal expertise
- Continual self-reflection and acquisition of skills
- Appropriate evaluation and use of research evidence in both basic and applied psychological science
- Understanding the influence of individual and cultural differences on treatment
- Seeking available resources (e.g., consultation, adjunctive or alternative services) as needed
- Having a cogent rationale for clinical strategies (APA, 2006)

Other disciplines have similarly developed definitions of EBP that increasingly involve factors such as clinical judgment, individual differences, and patient preference. The American Speech-Language-Hearing Association (ASHA) defines the goal of EBP as "the integration of (a) clinical expertise/expert opinion, (b) external scientific evidence, and (c) client/patient/caregiver perspectives to provide high-quality services reflecting the interests, values, needs, and choices of the individuals we serve" (ASHA Executive Board, 2004).

Despite the evolution in EBP toward greater consideration of interpersonal and personal components, the relative emphases on these factors versus emphasis on the range of research evidence is not agreed upon and continues to be hotly debated in research journals, in the clinical/educational domains, by proponents of specific methodologies, and by funders such as insurance companies. Summarizing the current state of uses of the term EBP as it pertains to autism treatment, Barry Prizant, a renowned researcher and clinician in the autism field, in his recent article on this topic, divides current uses into two categories:

> 1) EBP-A, to refer to the appropriate use of EBP as stipulated by accepted definitions of professional organizations noted above; and 2) the narrow use of EBP, which I will refer to as EBP-N, where sources of acceptable evidence are not only restricted to research considerations only (with client / family preferences virtually ignored), but also where the application of EBP goes well beyond clinical and educational decision-making to include or exclude funding of specific practices through political/legislative processes. (Prizant, 2011)

We are strong advocates of the current, broader use of EBP and our process throughout this book is based on this definition. The broader definition creates greater opportunity for treatment effectiveness in the face of ongoing evolution of the treatment field, whereas the narrower definition potentially hinders treatment progress and quality. However, even this broader definition leaves unanswered questions. What follows is a discussion of some of the complexities of the expanded definitions of EBP.

EBP as it Pertains to Autism

Balancing the more concrete issue of research rigor with the more subjective issues of, for example, client preference or clinical judgment, creates controversy regarding defining EBP in treating children with autism. This presents complicated challenges. We will briefly address these issues as follows.

Clinical Judgment

Although research syntheses of autism treatments conducted to develop EBP guidelines generally include a caveat that clinical judgment should also play a role in treatment selection, which clinicians' judgments should be taken into consideration? Equally important, which, if any, clinicians' judgments should be dismissed? On what basis should they make this judgment, and how should their judgment interface with research findings? These questions have not been given sufficient attention in the research or clinical literature. Most autism-specific treatment programs adhere to one model, approach, or philosophy, and consultation from colleagues within a particular program may help provide better services within that model, but they are unlikely to examine the utility of using components of another treatment model.

Some school systems use more eclectic approaches but employ staff who are not fully trained in any one approach. Few individuals have extensive training in multiple models and approaches. Many school systems have one autism consultant whose job it is to provide consultation to all staff members on every student with ASD, from the 4-year-old who is nonverbal and self-injurious to the teenager with Asperger's who is socially isolated and talking of suicide.

Clinicians as well as researchers in autism treatment often have strong biases. Very likely they are basing their opinions not only on the research they have reviewed but also on training and personal experience. One could argue that clinical judgment should incorporate the perspectives of clinicians with expertise both in a range of disciplines and in a range of treatment philosophies different from that of the primary clinician, classroom, or program. For example, if a child is in a program that uses approach X, and approach X isn't producing the expected gains, despite the efforts of a closely supervised, trained, and experienced treatment team delivering consistent services, the team may choose to consult a clinician with expertise in a different approach. This occurs infrequently. Those using approach X will usually stick with approach X. Many clinicians are unaware that there may be reasonable but very different alternative treatment approaches that could be more effective.

Autism-Specific Versus Nonspecific Treatments

The literature on EBP for children with autism generally includes autism-specific treatments and not treatments for the many common co-morbid conditions diagnosed in roughly 70% of children with autism. Cognitive-behavioral therapy (CBT) is, for example, an evidence-based treatment for children with anxiety, yet it hasn't been established as a treatment for children with autism *and* anxiety. Is it more consistent with EBP to consult the CBT literature and adapt for the child with ASD or to limit one's search to the ASD treatment literature? The former is more consistent with current conceptualization of EBP in terms of seeking treatment based on individual child characteristics.

The Evolution of Treatment Models and Terminology

Although there continues to be a need for any model to establish itself as effective for a specific population or problem through research findings, comparing treatments poses an enormous challenge because of the evolution of treatment models, with many combining and integrating components initially found only within one specific treatment. One would expect as a field progresses that professionals would develop new models, building on promising components of existing treatments. As this occurs, however, studies comparing treatment approaches quickly become outdated and of no use. For example, 10 years ago one could have conducted a study comparing Discrete Trial Training / ABA to Floortime™, but today a comparison study of behavioral versus developmental approaches would no longer be consistent with evaluating which approach is best, as several approaches with promising outcomes incorporate, each in different ways, components of both.

In "Joint Attention and Symbolic Play in Young Children with Autism: A Randomized Controlled Intervention Study" (Kasari, Freeman, & Paparella, 2006), a study conducted with research rigor sufficient to be included in several stringent EBP meta-analyses, a specific approach was found to significantly increase joint attention in the experimental group. The approach used, in combination with the other interventions both groups received, was described as a combination of "applied behavioral analysis and developmental procedures of responsive and facilitative interactive methods." In a meta-analysis one could interpret this study as supporting behavioral techniques or supporting developmental, relationship-based techniques, or both.

Relatedly, in a recent randomized controlled study (Dawson et al., 2010), the Early Start Denver Model was found to improve cognitive and adaptive skills and reduce severity of autism symptoms in toddlers. This model is described by the authors as a "comprehensive developmental behavioral intervention, merging components of developmental, relationship-based approaches with the behavioral approach of Pivotal Response Training" (Rogers and Dawson, 2009). Moreover, the very same treatment approach can be described in both behavioral and developmental terms. For example, a treater responding to a previously unresponsive 2-year-old who picks up a toy train by making train noises, smiling, and joining in the child's focus of interest to entice him to engage socially, may be described as a DIR®/Floortime™ approach, whereas another treater may call this ABA because she is positively reinforcing child's play by making the train noises the child has previously found motivating.

There is a role for multiple, detailed case studies tracking the nature of treatment rather than the philosophical underpinnings, and the process of progress during the course of treatment, focusing on the development of specific processes in well-characterized individual children in order to yield meaningful information regarding key active ingredients in treatment. One might find that different processes and different treatment ingredients were pivotal for different children.

Consider the following: A 3-year-old characterized as cognitively advanced but underaroused responds consistently to high-affect play, first with increased eye contact but not joint attention, and then, with careful environmental setup to promote and model joint attention, begins to initiate joint attention only during these sessions. Then three months later, he begins engaging in joint attention spontaneously in certain familiar situations. One might find another child, a 7-year-old who is globally delayed, already engaging in eye contact to share affect but who hasn't developed joint attention, even with environmental manipulations and interactive prompting. He begins to use joint attention only with his parents and only when playing on the sofa with one favorite toy through extensive modeling and prompting. With further intensive modeling and prompting, he expands this social game to include other adults and gradually to include other activities. So there is likely a different array of effective treatment strategies and developmental progressions for increasing acquisition of skills for different children.

Capturing these processes at the level of the individual child and treater would provide greater direction for treatment than large-scale group comparison studies of processes that involve many complex and varied developmental steps and manifestations across children. This approach would also be far more valid than the results of meta-analyses of studies of groups of children using different approaches, population characteristics, and so forth. Individual children are being treated, and a greater understanding of the processes of development in response to treatment of individual children would be a fruitful direction for research that could be of immediate use to treaters and their students, patients, and families.

A similar solution has been proposed, with some initial promising research work done at this level, regarding different treatment models (e.g., Psychodynamic Psychotherapy versus Cognitive Behavioral Therapy) for treating adult panic disorder (Ablon, Levy, & Katzenstein, 2006). Consulting meta-analyses of large-scale studies of children with autism can provide broad information, especially regarding general validity of treatment models, but these studies are less likely to inform specific treatment approaches for helping with specific challenges in complex individuals.

Client Voice in What to Treat and How to Treat

Involving clients in their own treatment process, including what they want help with and choice of treatment method, with continual evaluation and revision (e.g., Client-Directed Outcome-Informed Treatment, or CDOI), has been found to be a key component of effective treatment across several recent studies (e.g., Duncan, Miller, & Sparks, 2004). In work with clients who have typical communication and cognitive skills, several measures have been tested and used to conduct such studies. This is an exciting, promising development that cuts across many treatment modalities. However, treating individuals, many of whom can't speak for themselves, places extra responsibility on those devising and carrying out treatments to ensure their voices are somehow heard. Patients or students who don't have the cognitive or language ability to actively participate in the process are at greater risk for having treatments done *to them* instead of *with them*, and they are at greater risk for being subject to coercive, even harmful treatments. The U.S. Department of Justice's Investigation of the use of painful aversives at the Judge Rotenberg Center in Canton, Massachusetts, is one horrific example (Ahern & Rosenthal, 2008).

Treaters must continue to ask, "Is this the treatment this individual would choose if he or she were able to understand treatment choices, processes, and potential outcome(s)? Is this child satisfied with the treatment process and progress? Is there another treatment or are there changes in the current treatment that would make it more consistent with what the child would prefer, if he or she were able to express preferences?"

This issue has been addressed in a few ways in the autism treatment field. Embedding a requirement for working to maximize child motivation and enjoyment throughout teaching would seem to ensure that the child's "voice" is being heard within the treatment. This is not to say that a child must enjoy every aspect of treatment, but weighing child affect when making treatment selections would seem to be a key component in what is increasingly viewed as important in treatment outcome.

Several treatments, including DIR®/Floortime™, SCERTS™, RDI, and PRT, incorporate techniques for fostering positive child-adult interactions at their core. One treatment, the Early Start Denver Model, includes in their therapist Fidelity system a measure of how well the "Adult Optimizes Child Motivation for Participating in the Activity" (Rogers and Dawson, 2009). But measurements of child affect are often not included in autism treatment studies or meta-analyses.

Another way to ensure that patient, client, and student voices are heard in treatment choice and process is by including this element from the start, at the "identification of the problem" stage. This is similar to the CDOI model: What does the person to be treated want help with specifically? Schlosser, Koul, and Costello (2007) developed a model for selecting treatment in the Augmentative and Alternative Communication field, building on earlier models and adding the element of key stakeholder input. The addition of stakeholders refers to the individual's or client's perspective about what the problem is and how it should be treated, as well as the input of those with whom the person communicates.

Striving to attain positive child affect toward and during treatment should be intrinsic to treatment, and it should have primacy over other components of EBP in treatment selection. For example, let's say one is working with a child who has a very limited diet, rejects any new food, and whose pediatrician is concerned about his growth and nutrition. The treatment team may review the literature and come across a review of treatments for food selectivity in children with ASD (Volkert & Vaz, 2010) in a reputable source, the *Journal of Applied Behavior Analysis*. In it, the authors cite two studies as offering promising approaches to be further explored:

> For example, Patel et al. (2007) presented high-probability demands (three presentations of an empty spoon) followed by a low-probability demand (a spoon with food) to increase the food acceptance of a young child with pervasive developmental disorder. Future studies should replicate and extend those of Patel et al. with a larger group of children with autism.

And Bachmeyer et al. (2009)

> used escape extinction (non-removal of the spoon) and attention extinction (no differential consequence for inappropriate mealtime behavior) individually and in combination with four children whose inappropriate mealtime behavior was maintained by escape and attention. Attention extinction alone did not decrease inappropriate mealtime behavior or increase acceptance. By contrast, escape extinction alone decreased inappropriate mealtime behavior and increased acceptance. However, combined attention and escape extinction resulted in further decreases in inappropriate mealtime behavior and increases in the stability of acceptance relative to escape extinction alone.

We would posit that, if given a voice (the ability to express a preference), the child would probably not choose either of these treatments if other more pleasurable and effective treatments were available. There is no measure of child affect during these treatments, but logic would suggest that the positive outcome was achieved because of the aversive experience of the alternative condition to eating. What if no other treatments have this level of research backing? Should the clinician reject other approaches?

Giving priority to the patient voice, one would first consider treatments that the child would enjoy, such as using behavioral principles by pairing eating a less-preferred item with a happy adult-child engagement. If the child enjoys singing, one could pair the spoon near the child's lips with the exciting part of the song and pair the child making increasing approximations to trying the new food with the onset of the fun part of the song. One could also consider treatments that are successful for other populations to overcome previously aversive experiences (e.g., CBT to treat specific phobias) and adapt these treatments to this population.

We have developed a treatment, "Replays" (Levine & Chedd, 2007), which has only anecdotal and case study support, yet is highly pleasurable to children and caregivers. It is also based on the rigorously research-supported principle of Exposure Response Prevention (ERP). One could try this approach first, pretending the adult or a doll tries the food and spits it out or whatever the child already does, in a playful manner, saying "Yucky," again in a playful fashion, trying small variations until one has the child's attention and the child is laughing. Repeating this enjoyable routine numerous times can desensitize the child to his learned pattern of rejecting food, as he forms a new learned pairing of fun, happy social play to being offered food, resulting in a positive experience based in ERP. Such an approach, which has embedded in it child positive affect, would take precedence as a first-line approach to try, rather than first relying on two studies that have success but also include an aversive child experience as the mechanism of change.

Children with autism and other developmental disabilities are more vulnerable to being treated with less pleasurable approaches than other populations, because they are less able to speak for themselves. Again, the onus is even more on the practitioner as well as the researcher to incorporate positive child experience into treatment approaches.

Family Preferences

Statements regarding the importance of including families in treatments and involving them in treatment choice (Koegel, Vernon, & Koegel, 2009) can be found repeatedly throughout the autism treatment literature. Families' preferences may be substituted for child preferences, which may be appropriate for very young children and those who lack the cognitive or communicative capacity to participate in this process. One team was working with a 7-year-old boy with Down syndrome and autism on dressing, toileting, and independent feeding skills, and he was making major gains at school but not at home. The team was growing increasingly frustrated with the family for not following through. The family was growing increasingly frustrated, too, and wondered why the program wasn't making their child more social. The program staff and family met, and it became clear that the strongest priority for this family was social skills, specifically to have their child look at them and develop sounds and words for their names and to say "Mommy." The program staff shifted their priorities. Although they didn't stop working to develop more independence in the boy's self-care skills, they built more social language and interactions into their routine.

In another situation, a preschooler's treatment team was working "full throttle" in teaching compliance. Specifically, the classroom teacher wanted the child to sit for circle time and snack. When he didn't follow the rules, he would lose recess time, just as his classmates would if they didn't follow the rules, which led to further tantruming. The team felt they were making agonizingly slow progress and had weeks and weeks of data sheets to prove it. When they brought up this fact at a team meeting, the child's parents admitted that they don't require their child to sit during meals or in any group situations, because it was always such an ordeal. He would yell, bolt, or even throw food. It was fine with them if he ate a sandwich in an adjoining room with his favorite video playing while they enjoyed a peaceful meal. They fully understood the team's emphasis on the importance of behaving at school and wanted to support the school team's efforts, but they insisted that he not be "punished" for leaving snack or circle. The school team agreed to rewrite the plan and reinstituted recess. They also added music and silly, playful elements to both snack and circle as incentives. The parents agreed to follow the new protocol, first around sitting for meals and then for staying in a group—at a birthday party or at their church daycare—for increasingly longer periods. Over the course of several weeks, the child's willingness to sit improved both in and out of school. Subsequently, the family and school team kept in closer touch regarding goals, preferences, and any shift in priorities.

What Is Important to Study? What Is Important to Treat?

There is likely a bias in what is studied in the autism treatment research field. Treatments that generate quantified data on factors that are easily measurable lend themselves more readily to research than do treatments that do not generate data, those that generate qualitative data, or those that treat difficult-to-measure but very important dependent variables (e.g., family well-being, a child's happiness, a child's feeling of being liked by peers, a teenager's feeling of belonging, a child's or family's sense of hope and optimism).

In each of the seminal iterations of EBP or relatedly, the comprehensive meta-analyses of the research literature that have been developed (APA, 2006; Rogers & Vismara, 2008; National Standards Project, 2010), what has been most debated and revised is what constitutes valid research methodology. What constitutes social relevance, while addressed in each of these and several other formulations of EBP, should be at the helm of treatment discussions and has been given insufficient attention. Several clinical models include factors related to positive child affect, child motivation, and teaching key skills to improve quality of life, but these factors have not been given front-line consideration in most treatment literature meta-analyses that offer conclusions and recommendations for best practices.

Which dependent variables should be looked at? We would give priority to studies that identify and clearly define the following as dependent variables:

- Improvement in child affect, emotional regulation, happiness, and well-being
- Increase in social overtures and the capacity to and interest in sustaining social engagement across a range of affective states and interactive situations
- Improvement in functioning in daily living and self care
- Improvement in family well-being

We believe that studies with dependent variables that provide measures of these factors offer greater validity than do studies that use "improvement in IQ scores" or improvement on any standardized test that doesn't also measure improvement in actual functioning in an area related to quality of life. The factors we emphasize enhance the quality of life for all of us—those who have autism as well as those who don't—and should be given high priority in determining which studies should be included in any meta-analysis and in evaluating specific studies.

Even with these priorities, a multistep process may be needed to determine what to treat and how to treat it. Although this approach sounds obvious, treatments are often applied because they have been found effective, but not in treating the actual cause of the problem one is targeting. If the treatment is working slowly or not at all, the problem could be, not in the treatment, but in the determination of what the problem is. One may be treating a child who bolts by rewarding him for staying in class, with little or no positive impact, only to find out that, when the class was temporarily moved to a different part of the building because of construction, he did not bolt. In such a case, it turned out, after many trials and processes of elimination, that the ticking of an old electric clock in the original classroom was highly aversive to the child.

In another situation, a very anxious child with PDD-NOS was being treated for feeding issues. He didn't like to eat, had a very limited diet, and was rapidly losing weight. He had a thorough medical workup and no problems were identified. One doctor recommended a feeding tube, which his parents wanted to avoid. The behavior consultant tried several common treatments, consulted with feeding specialists, an occupational therapist, and another behavior specialist, and worked closely with his parents but still made no headway. Ultimately, when the child's medical team did a more invasive workup, they uncovered a medical problem that impacted feeding and appetite. It was surgically repaired, and the previously unsuccessful feeding treatments were reinstituted. His appetite and enjoyment of eating gradually increased, and he began gaining weight.

The Role of Context in Treatment Selection

Treatments occur at home, in schools, in clinics, and in the community. Sometimes a treatment that seems like the best option based on research and clinical judgment may not be a good choice because of family or patient factors. A family that greatly values academic achievement over play may have little interest in their 10-year-old with Asperger's developing pretend play skills, even though his clinician might have determined this would be helpful to him. A family struggling to make it through sleepless nights and days of tantrums may not be interested in or able to carry over a treatment to teach reading, even though the child's teacher feels that this is an important goal and needs to be worked on at home. A labor-intensive behavior plan that is based on sound research and is working at school may be impossible for a family to carry out if there are three other children with special needs in the family and one parent working two jobs to make ends meet. One must weigh these sorts of contextual factors against other evidence in selecting treatments.

Positive and Negative Policy Implications of Uses of EBP in Autism Treatments

In August 2010, a new law was passed in Massachusetts, House Bill 4935, making it the 23rd state to adopt the Act Relative to Insurance Coverage for Autism (ARICA). This bill mandates that health insurers cover services not previously covered, including home-based treatments by paraprofessionals, supervised by professionals. It is largely the result of widespread advocacy efforts, but also research studies finding that intensive home-based services for children with ASD are ultimately both effective and also cost effective. However, at this time some insurance providers are specifying that the treatment must be supervised by a Board-Certified Behavior Analyst (BCBA). This is also based on the large body of studies of ABA treatments having what was perceived as more or stronger convincing evidence, as measured in a variety of different ways in different studies, than studies of other treatments such as DIR®/Floortime™, RDI, SCERTS™, or the Early Start Denver Model, all of which also have studies supporting their efficacy. Only treatment that comes under the category of ABA has been authorized to be covered by some of the insurance plans. Therefore, if a clinician is certified through any of these other treatment certification processes, which each of these other approaches also has, but not by the Behavior Analyst Certification Board (BACB), they are deemed by these insurance plans as not qualified to supervise paraprofessionals.

This greatly limits family choice and individualization of treatment to match the child's needs, and it completely eliminates the role of clinical judgment. So the power of the evidence from treatment research provided much support in enacting a law to require insurance coverage for more treatment for children and families. Yet the use of an extremely narrow definition of EBP significantly limits which treatment approach is considered worthy of being covered.

For families/children for whom the ABA treatment (or any other treatment) is not consistent with their own values or with the clinical judgment of treaters, or the treating clinicians' interpretation of available research literature as it pertains to the individual child's needs, the services covered are not consistent with the current definition of EBP. For example, a 15-year-old boy with Asperger's and depression who is socially isolated, grieving the loss of a parent, and acting out in school may have a behavior plan developed to treat his acting-out behavior, even when there is no evidence that current treatment for grief and depression in teenagers with Asperger's should be based in ABA. The cause of his acting out may be better treated by ensuring that he has more social engagement, social skills training, grief counseling adapted to his needs, and/or support in friendship development. Moreover, the APA-recommended treatment for depression is cognitive-behavior therapy (www.apa.org/divisions/div12/rev_est/anxiety.html#gad). Typically, someone with a BCBA credential would not necessarily have training in CBT, as it is not required for certification, unless this was another area of specialty or a particular interest.

When only one treatment model is supported by a funding agency, providers have to make a choice between providing needed services for families who may not otherwise be able to afford services, perhaps deciding that this treatment is preferable to no treatment, even if this treatment approach is not entirely consistent with EBP. Use of one model for a given child may not be consistent with clinical judgment, family values, child-specific factors, or relevant research.

Conclusions and Recommendations

What is the teacher or clinician or parent to do in the face of such complexity and so many unanswered questions? The fact is that we will not be able to answer this in a concrete, absolute manner. For each child, the answer will be individualized. Moreover, the answer may change over time, just as children with autism and their needs, circumstances, and capabilities change over time. Furthermore, new treatments and new variations of current treatments are continually being developed. We believe it is important to understand and accept this uncertainty, to carry on with an increasingly informed and open mind, and to continue to focus on the child and the problem, examining all components of EBP, and monitoring and reassessing strategies over time, rather than assuming that any one treatment approach will be the best practice for all children at all stages of their development.

In the next chapter we describe our process for planning and implementing treatment using EBP.

CHAPTER 3

THE INDIVIDUALIZED, PROBLEM-SOLVING TREATMENT PROCESS

This process for planning and implementing treatment using EBP draws on many approaches, but it may be most similar to the one posed by Mesibov and Shea (2011). These authors summarize the view of the state of EBP and autism treatment this way:

> Assessing the evidence base of an intervention or program is particularly complex when there are multiple forms of evidence to consider. What to do when a study's results are statistically significant but clinically questionable? What to do when an intervention is highly regarded clinically but has a relatively small research base? What to do when a dubious commercial program documents tremendous parental support? Perhaps clinicians and educators in the area of autism would do well to consider the legal concept of the "preponderance of the evidence." That is, rather than trying to identify the "truth," we should recognize that there are several legitimate but potentially conflicting or incomplete sources of information. Our charge is to consider the various forms of evidence and make judgments about what approaches seem most reasonable, recognizing that our knowledge is imperfect, that generally effective approaches sometimes fail and unlikely

approaches sometimes succeed, and that all intervention principles and techniques must ultimately be individualized to each client or student and then assessed for effectiveness in that unique situation. (p. 127).

The Process:

1. Is based in careful consideration of the problem one is treating or aspect one is targeting, formulated in conjunction with key stakeholders, including the child and family whenever possible

2. Places great value on familiarity with the individual child's characteristics, likes, dislikes, learning processes and style, and family/cultural context, in addition to the broad, multifaceted components of an autism diagnosis

3. Prioritizes treatment selection and modification based on progress toward specific goals in a context that maximizes child positive and/or well regulated affect and motivation for participation

4. Gives considerable weight to clinical judgment of experienced professionals from a diverse range of areas of expertise

5. Incorporates approaches consistent with what has been found to be effective for similar children in similar contexts for similar problems, as long as those approaches also incorporate principles 1 to 4

6. Closely monitors treatment impact and adjusts according to all of the above principles

7. Places emphasis on seeking treatment that maximizes child well-being

8. Places emphasis on seeking treatments wherein fostering social and emotional engagement is a priority, and a context for teaching

9. Does not use techniques that are known to cause harm

The expanded conceptualization of EBP is becoming increasingly related to what is likely to be the most effective way of doing treatment. That is, careful formulation of the problem one is treating, in what context, and with what individual characteristics and qualities is a vital step driving the rest of the process. Best practices are the result of an interpretation of evidence bearing on treatment planning that incorporates patient (child, family) involvement in treatment choice, initially and over time, sound, informed clinical judgment, findings from single-case design research in addition to other forms of research including randomized controlled trials, treatment models that are not just autism specific when treating co-morbid conditions, monitoring treatment outcome, and making adjustments as one proceeds (i.e., practice-based evidence).

Our Beliefs and Biases

It is clear to anyone reviewing autism treatment models, research articles, or observing children in treatment programs and schools that there are many differences of opinion about how to treat children with autism, even children who have similar profiles and are struggling with similar issues. Clinicians, teachers, parents, those who develop treatment models, and those who study them all have their own lenses through which they interpret information based on their experiences, training, treatment context, and other factors, such as their own personalities, social skills, learning style, and even their most basic philosophical beliefs.

In working with individual children, or writing about working with individual children, it is impossible to be objective, to have no values or opinions. Thus, it is important to be aware of one's values and opinions rather than work or write as if one were valueless or objective. Making these values explicit helps others put one's work into context. Furthermore, as the model of EBP illustrated throughout this book is based in part on the impact of people's (i.e., providers', families', children's) beliefs, opinions, or experiences regarding treatment, it is important to clearly state our own beliefs. These are, like our EBP process, based on an integration of a range of sources of evidence: specifically, our interpretation of several bodies of research (e.g., autism treatment literature, child development literature, family therapy and psychotherapy treatment literature, anxiety treatment literature); each of our own 20-plus years of clinical experience with children with autism and their families, in homes, hospital clinics, Early Intervention programs, schools, and private practice; our own diverse autism-specific training in DIR®/Floortime™ and other developmental, relationship-based approaches as well as in Applied Behavioral Analysis; our backgrounds as mental health professionals (Chedd's degree in Mental Health Counseling and Levine's degree in Developmental Psychology); our life experiences and roles as parents; and our development and use of a model that is enjoyable for both adults and children (Affective Behavioral Play Therapy) for treating specific phobias and behavioral challenges in young children with ASD (Levine & Chedd, 2007), as well as Levine's background in codeveloping a model of drama-based social pragmatics for teens with Asperger's disorder (Lerner, Mikami, & Levine, 2010).

We base our process on a combination of and interplay among research findings, beliefs, and experiences. Perhaps most important, treatment can and should maximize a child's positive, affective participation. Teaching is more effective when a child's emotional system is positively engaged. Specific goals, such as teaching socially shared, positive affect, and initiation of joint attention, have been found to more rapidly develop overt targeting of positive child affect (Landa, Holman, O'Neill, & Stuart, 2011). Conversely, behavioral challenges are more likely to occur in children who are depressed (Magnuson & Constantino, 2011). We also believe that helping a child to sustain an emotionally regulated and functional state and an interactive state across a range of emotions (e.g., sadness, anxiety, anger) is also vital.

Our emphasis in this discussion on positive affect is in reference to the child's overall orientation to the treatment process, rather than on specific goals of helping children learn to cope increasingly adaptively with a full range of emotions, which is also vital. However, an overall positive emotional orientation during the treatment process is more likely to lead to treatment success, is a necessary component in providing humane, socially just treatment, and is especially important when treating individuals with diminished capacity to speak for themselves regarding treatment participation and choice.

The Role of Children's Emotions

It is important to consider the role of children's emotions in treatment planning, although it is not always easy or possible to measure/quantify. Helping children develop the ability to regulate emotionally across an increasing range of circumstances and especially helping children to experience a sense of well-being, to be happy as a general state, are important goals. Depression and anxiety are common co-morbidities in this population and are highly correlated with increases in a variety of behavioral challenges (Magnuson & Constantino, 2011).

Often an artificial divide exists in both the clinical and research literature and fields, between methodologies considered Behavioral/ABA, as referring to those with data collection/thorough progress monitoring, specific goal scope and sequences, techniques such as least-to-most prompting, task analysis, backwards chaining, and Antecedent-Behavior-Consequence or ABC teaching, as opposed to models that are considered developmental and/or relationship-based. The principles often associated with ABA are, in fact, incorporated into many different treatment models, including those associated with increasing positive child affect, socially shared joint attention, social reciprocity, and social initiation. These include DIR®/Floortime™, The Early Start Denver Model (ESDM), Pivotal Response Training (PRT), Relationship Development

Intervention (RDI), and the SCERTS Model, among others. (See Appendix A for a description of these models.)

The inverse of this is not necessarily the case. That is, treatment models labeled as ABA, especially older models with a major emphasis on Discrete Trial Training (DTT), for instance, often do not target as an outcome factors such as child positive affect, emotional regulation, initiation of social joint attention, or expanding social reciprocity. Newer models generally considered within the ABA umbrella, including Positive Behavioral Supports (PBS), PRT, and the ESDM, place enormous emphasis on those factors. For a still conceptually applicable, although older discussion framing treatments into a continuum, see Prizant and Wetherby (1998). All of these approaches have a research base. The challenge is making decisions about which approach(es) to use, how, and with whom.

The Challenge of Generalization

Goals are more likely to be generalized when taught in a context that is familiar or meaningful to the child and within a flow of interaction. Teaching isolated facts or skills out of context, a practice often used in DTT, especially to a population known to have difficulty with generalizing, may result in an increase in a child's mastery of these rote skills in a particular setting, but it does not meet our standards of effective or meaningful teaching for all children in all circumstances.

For example, DTT can be very effective in teaching numbers and one-to-one correspondence or colors or specific vocabulary but not necessarily how and when to use these words and concepts, particularly in a social situation that necessitates spontaneous conversation. Treatment must also be consistent with family style and preferences in order to maximize family participation in treatment and treatment effectiveness. A very organized, methodical family with a predictable schedule may welcome step-by-step instructions and data collection sheets. A more free-spirited family, one that enjoys novelty, spontaneity, and has less clearly defined roles and varying schedules may find such an approach too rigid and constraining. A family in the midst of chaos and multiple high-demand situations may experience such a program as an added demand and hence be less likely to follow instructions. In theory a picture schedule, for example, might be helpful for a child in all of these situations. But if a picture schedule is not viewed as useful by the families, they are not likely to use it.

Strengthening Social Connections

Goals related to improving quality of life for the child and family are vital in treatment. Social isolation is common in children and teens with ASD and can lead to loneliness, depression, and other emotional and behavioral consequences (Bauminger & Kasari, 2003; Whitehouse, Durkin, Jaquet, & Ziatas, 2009). So treatments that directly increase skills that contribute to the child's capacity to engage in personally and emotionally meaningful social interactions and are likely to lead to stronger peer relationships and friendship development across ages and across the spectrum are of great importance for quality of life. This is beneficial, not only to the child undergoing treatment, but for the entire family.

We provide a process for working in a manner consistent with EBP for those working with children with ASD. The nine case studies that are included demonstrate how practitioners have used this model and the complexities of doing so. These case studies are intended to illustrate ways to use this process beginning from scratch or incorporating it into an existing treatment plan. It is one process for decision making, treatment selections, and implementation, rather than a comprehensive guide to treatment for all children with autism spectrum disorders, which, at this point in the development of the field, would not be possible.

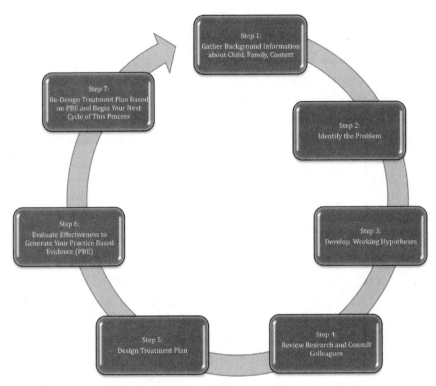

Figure 3.1 Individualized Treatment Planning Process

Step 1: Gather Background Information

Before deciding on specific interventions, you need to address and attempt to answer several questions: Who is the child being treated and in what context? In order to develop an effective treatment plan, it is imperative to not only understand the child's diagnosis but to know the individual child. You will want to find out about his strengths, interests, likes, and dislikes. Why are such details important? If he has a dog and is comfortable around animals, you may want to include toy animals, pictures of animals, and animal sounds in your treatment routines. You may even want to include his dog! Or work to develop an interest in his peers' pets. Conversely, if he is frightened of dogs or dislikes loud noises, especially barking, you will focus on very different themes and props, or it may be important to treat his fear of dogs, if many of his neighbors and relatives have dogs.

Keep Asking Questions

Answering as many questions as you can about the child's background will also inform the way you present treatment options— the simplicity or complexity of the language you use, how and at what pace you introduce the details of the treatment plan, and how you describe the treatment process and expectations, both the family's and your own. For example, if you are working with a child whose parents are fluent English speakers and are professionals in a medical field, you may use different language when you talk about the specifics of autism. In contrast, defining and describing autism to parents of a child from a culture that doesn't have a word for autism will require different language (and an interpreter if possible) and the use of familiar analogies and examples drawn from that culture. Although the emotional content of your words may be the same, the actual words and descriptions may be, appropriately, quite different, in order to communicate similar meanings to both families.

Does the child have any known medical conditions? If she has a chronic illness, even something as common as frequent colds or ear infections, she may see many medical professionals on a regular basis. She may associate one more professionals (you) with uncomfortable injections, being poked and prodded, having to wait in brightly lit or strange-smelling exam rooms—or something else that has caused distress or discomfort. Her family, understandably, may be more focused on medical well-being and less on developmental treatment at a particular point in time. It's important to take into account such issues and especially the family's priorities.

Has he experienced any major changes, trauma, or significant loss? Maybe your client has recently moved, has a new baby sister, or has experienced the departure of a long-term caregiver such as an aunt or babysitter. Or he may have experienced a major disruption or dramatic event, such as a fire in his house, the military deployment of one parent, or the serious illness of a grandparent.

What are his living arrangements? A two-parent family in which only one parent works full time with a single child may have more time and flexibility than a single parent of three, working as a nurse on the night shift. The same is true for parents who have lived in the same neighborhood for a long time and have extended family or friends close by who can help with childcare and chores. They may be able to spend more hours working directly with their child and implementing techniques they have learned through observation or direct teaching than the family who recently arrived from another state or another country, who have no local family and are just learning to access community resources. Taking into consideration details and differences such as these will lead to more realistic and useful goals and a greater likelihood of achieving those goals.

Whose Priorities?

How do the child's caregivers feel about her and what do they prioritize for her development? What do they believe about treatment for her? The answers to these questions are of major importance, too. What is problematic for one parent, such as a child's not talking, may not concern another parent because "all the boys in my family were late talkers." Or a mother might be desperate to hear her child call "Mommy" from the next room, or say "I love you" and have little concern about her daughter's entering kindergarten knowing how to count to 10 or identifying five colors.

It is also important to know the child's treatment history. What has or hasn't worked in the past? How did the child respond? If a family has had a negative experience with a particular treatment approach or individual treater, you may run into some resistance and find it difficult to get them engaged in treatment again, even if your style or approach is completely different. Similarly, if a family is convinced that there is one way to treat a specific problem (e.g., by instituting a very strict diet or vitamin regimen), particularly one you believe to be without merit in treating the problem, you may find it equally challenging to introduce a treatment program with a solid research base that you believe has a good chance for solving a specific problem.

Making the Right Match

Getting to know the child's personality and style may help you make adjustments in your own style that will lead to a more positive outcome. Has there been any pattern or specific barriers to successful development (e.g., difficulty with mood regulation or extreme rigidity)? If the child needs a great deal of time to get accustomed to a new person or routine or has frequent upsets, you will need to build more time into the program so you can introduce new tasks at a slower pace.

Maybe there have been major strengths and advantages in the treatment process in the past, such as strong family involvement. You will know you can assign homework and the family will carry out the program with enthusiasm, perhaps leading to more rapid success.

Starting in the Middle

What type of program is he in now? How long has he been in this program? If the child has happily and willingly participated in the program, it is more likely that he will be open to another program and treater. But if you are, for example, taking over the role of a treater with whom the child has formed a strong bond, you may also find that it will take longer to build a positive, trusting working relationship.

How do the key people in his life—family, doctors, therapists, and school staff—understand this child, and how do they view what is or isn't helpful to him? Most people have heard or read something about autism, whether or not they work in the field or have had direct contact with someone with ASD. And they may have strong opinions about which type of treatment is or isn't appropriate. However, be sure to take very seriously the experiences of others who know the child well. Listen to how they describe the child's reactions and responses. A father may tell you that it's difficult to get his son to engage in toy play, but that he absolutely loves playing chase, tickling, and wrestling, and that he vocalizes more and makes better eye contact during active, outdoor play. Or a babysitter might share with you that the child seems far less agitated and more willing to engage when she and other adults talk quietly and keep a bit more physical distance, rather than getting close and coming on strong. These are important cues that you need to consider as you begin your work with the child and family. Even if you have worked with children with similar problems and have had success with a particular approach, you need to pay close attention to this child's and these parents' reactions.

Although it is impossible to find out everything about every child, family, and school, these issues—and many others that will come up during observation and discussions with the child's family throughout the course of treatment—will have a bearing on the direction your treatment plan takes, including the outcome. You may find as you proceed, especially if your treatment isn't resulting in the expected gains as you gather your practice-based evidence, that revisiting your initial questioning process may lead to acquiring more fruitful and previously overlooked information.

Step 2: Identify the Problem

This may be stating the obvious, but it is worth asking, "What is this child doing (or not doing) that is problematic? It may be a problem associated with and typical within the diagnosis, such as limited expressive or receptive communication skills, a behavioral challenge, or an inability to engage in imaginary play. Or it may be a problem with a possible biological component, such as refusing to eat or an inability to ever sleep through the night. In many cases there are multiple factors contributing to the problem, which will make it more difficult to treat, and it might take longer than anticipated. Nevertheless, the more precisely you can describe the problem, the more successful you will be at coming up with a reasonable plan to address it.

Often there is one primary problem, but it may be manifesting differently at different times, or in different settings. Or there may be several problems that need to be addressed at the same time. If you are targeting a behavior problem, you will want to find out if it occurs at school, at home, or both. Or does it occur in other environments, like only on community outings—to the grocery store or the park? Or perhaps it occurs only when the child is transitioning from one setting to another but does not happen once the child is settled into a routine. Maybe the problem occurs everywhere but only under particular circumstances. For example, the child may be calm and regulated most of the time but screams and gets aggressive if another person—a teacher or even Grandma—gets too close, touches him, or picks him up without sufficient warning.

Identifying Onset May Lead to a Quicker Solution

Can you pinpoint when the problem began? If you are focusing more on a developmental roadblock, try to recall or find out from others when it first become apparent or problematic (e.g., a child who isn't developing language despite developmental gains in motor and self-help skills). You will also want to determine who is affected and especially who is disturbed by the problem. If there is more than one problem, it will help to prioritize and determine which one to focus on first. You may find that solving one problem may solve or at least alleviate another. For example, a nonverbal 2-year-old refuses to eat, throws food, and constantly cries at mealtimes, and you determine that the cause may be her inability to express which foods she wants and doesn't want. Teaching her to use a simple picture communication system to identify preferred foods will lead to better eating behavior and fewer emotional outbursts. Or a 6-year-old insists on being first, in every situation—in the classroom, lunchroom, on the playground. His classmates avoid him during recess, and he is becoming more and more withdrawn. A combination of designing a behavior plan that reinforces taking turns and teaching him a few key phrases, such as "You go first. Then I'll go," and "I'll go after you," and also supporting his social interactions draws classmates to him; his sadness and isolation decrease; and his insistance on being first also decreases.

"But He Never Does This at School ..."

You need to determine early on for whom the problem is a problem. You may discover that the same behavior is considered a problem in one situation but not in another. For example, a child is not expected to sit for mealtimes at home; his parents have opposite work schedules and his much older siblings are in and out of the house constantly. So everyone eats "on the fly." In contrast, everyone in the child's second-grade class is expected to eat snack and lunch together at the same table and ask permission before getting out of their seats. So every snack and lunchtime results in the child's getting up multiple times and the teachers' frustration. "Why doesn't he listen to us?" they might ask. "Why can't he learn to follow directions, like everyone else?" Or perhaps the child, who is verbal but not very communicative, gets many food choices at snacktime at school, but at home, it's either a piece of fresh fruit or raisins and neither are exciting, compared to graham cracker bears, granola bars, or pink yogurt in a colorful tube. So snacktime at home almost always ends up in an argument and tears. His parents conclude, wrongly, that he is hopelessly picky or worse, intentionally noncompliant. Questions about the specifics of snacktime may not come up at a parent-teacher conference, and a problem with a reasonably simple solution (parents and school staff agree on which snacks they will and won't offer) may continue.

Input From Key Players

Most adults have theories or beliefs about many aspects of a child, including how they learn, how fast they acquire skills, the causes of their maladaptive behaviors, and what approaches will lead to better behaviors. Often these theories differ between home and school, between different members of a treatment team, even between parents. So it will be helpful to gather information from each of the key players about their understanding of how the child "ticks," as well as information specific to what one is treating.

Consider the father who believes his son is being "willfully defiant" when he refuses to brush his teeth, and tries various means to get his cooperation, including withholding all sweets or taking away TV time. He believes that his son *should* and *will* learn to brush his teeth if he is deprived. This is perhaps how he was raised and how he raised his other children and it worked well. However, for this child, none of these sanctions work, and in fact, his son's behavior becomes far worse. He used to simply refuse to brush his teeth. Now he is screaming and spitting, then bolting from the bathroom! His mother, after having several conversations about toothbrushing with their 5-year-old's school team and particularly his OT, who conducts various experiments about the child's preferences resulting in a comprehensive sensory profile, comes up with the solution: blue toothpaste and a musical, electric toothbrush lead to consistent, independent toothbrushing twice a day and much happier family interactions.

Step 3: State the Hypothesis, Yours and Others'

"You" refers to you, the consultant or principal, the teacher or therapist, the parent or the paraprofessional—anyone who is contributing to developing the treatment plan. You probably have some idea about what may be causing this problem and about why this child is behaving this way. Maybe he cries a lot because he needs something he is not getting—food, a particular toy, attention from a certain adult or peer, or more playtime. Maybe he hits the children next to him because he doesn't like where he has to sit at circle time; his spot is too close to the door, or not close enough. Or possibly he looks sad more often than not because he's cold or his shirt is itchy, or because he's tired of spending recess walking around the playground alone. There are many possible explanations, and different people are likely to have differing beliefs based on their experiences with the child and what they have observed, their biases and beliefs about this child, about autism, and about treatment. So it is important to have discussions with as many of them as you can, or better, to convene the child's entire team.

In addition to the background information you have already collected and your own theories, you will want to talk with the other providers who are working with or have recently evaluated this child, or have in the past, if it is possible. At the very least, you will want to review written assessments and progress reports. These may give you information that is not obvious or that brings to light changes in the child's life that may have led to the current problem. In the beginning stages of treatment plan development, looking at the situation from many angles and working to obtain or develop multiple hypotheses is likely to be most effective. This fosters broad-based observation and collection of potentially relevant information and forces you to avoid zeroing in on what may turn out to be irrelevant details and unintentionally overlooking what may turn out to be the key components. In the previous toothbrushing example, it might have been more effective and ultimately, would have saved more time and tears if all major stakeholders—the child's parents, classroom teacher, OT, physician, school behavioral consultant, and even his siblings—speculated on what might be the cause of his refusal to brush his teeth, rather than going with one person's assumption and treating it in one manner.

FBAs Provide Valuable Information

Clearly, multiple sources of information inform initial hypotheses about how best to help a child advance or resolve a behavioral challenge, including observations, information from those who know the child best, record reviews, and consideration of past history. For specific behavioral challenges, consider conducting a comprehensive Functional Behavioral Assessment (FBA). This process incorporates many techniques—interviews, observation, recording incidences of specific behaviors in specific contexts, analyzing data, and evaluating outcomes—to determine why a child is behaving in a particular way. That is, is there a situation or one component of a situation that is causing the child distress? Or is the child obtaining a desired outcome as a result of his behavior in certain circumstances? Once the cause or purpose of the (usually maladaptive) behavior has been determined, a plan for helping the child develop more adaptive, socially acceptable ways of expressing this same need or coping with the same situation can be put in place. For example, a child who is anxious and becomes disruptive when math class begins, knowing he will be sent to the principal's office and thus escape from math, can learn to ask for help with his work or a break, using verbal or nonverbal means. Or changes can be made in a program such that the child no longer needs to behave inappropriately (e.g., if the child is screaming because his seat is next to a noisy air vent, his seat can be moved).

This may sound like a simple procedure, but it is not. A good FBA takes into account the observations of a child over several settings and over a reasonable amount of time. How much time? There is no perfect amount, but it should be sufficient to get a sampling of behaviors under different conditions, such as in different classrooms, with different teachers, at home when the child is well rested and maybe when he is tired, and perhaps in other environments, such as the library or playground. Determining where, how, and when to record observational data will depend largely on where the behavior is likely to occur—and possibly where it is least likely to occur. (For additional information on FBAs, see Appendix A.)

At this stage, you may come up with one or possibly several hypotheses. Consider the following scenario: "Our 2-year-old has major tantrums during just about every meal. Her speech is limited, and she has no reliable way to ask for what she needs. Maybe she wants something different to eat or drink or a favorite cup. Or maybe she doesn't want to stop what she's doing or she wants more (or not so much) attention." So one of the major goals will be to develop a functional communication system and teach her how to use it. Or this one: "We've been working in class on developing language for over a year with no progress. She doesn't talk to or interact with her classmates." To begin you will want to look at what approaches and systems have been used to help her acquire language and especially explore how much receptive language she has. You will also want to consider if treatment in other areas has been successful, which may provide clues as to how she learns, and also look at if and how she is communicating in other settings. Or "He only bites his hand after he's been sitting in the same place for more than 15 minutes or when his teacher or mother is talking to someone else." Again, there are several possibilities. He may be restless and needs to move around. Or he may be confused because his understanding of spoken language is limited. He may be bored and has no ability to entertain himself or self-soothe. Or he may have found that biting his hand is a sure way to gain much-wanted adult attention. Another situation: "He speaks a lot at home but never at school." He is in a large class, has a skilled teacher and very involved parents, is bilingual, and anxious, so something or several factors may be contributing to his lack of speech in the classroom, and it isn't yet clear what those factors are. In all these situations, many hypotheses can be developed.

The Blame Game

While it can be tempting, and sometimes warranted, to dismiss unlikely sounding or blame-oriented hypotheses, it can also be extremely helpful to at least gather key people's private hypotheses. Sometimes the hunch or gut feeling of someone who spends the most time with the child may have validity, as it may be based on a great deal of observation and interaction. But it may also be given less credibility because it comes from a source with less formal autism-related education (e.g., an aide, a babysitter, a sibling). And sometimes private hypotheses are based on blaming other parties (e.g., "He behaves badly because his parents never set limits," or "She has no speech because the school doesn't know how to teach her," both of which may or may not be accurate). Being aware of and exploring each hypothesis when appropriate can be enormously helpful in providing a context for developing and implementing an appropriate treatment plan that all stakeholders will find valid and support.

There are situations in which one or more members of a child's team have a hypothesis that blames the child ("He doesn't do the work because he is lazy"). This explanation may make most parents and educators cringe, but this stakeholder's perspective is helpful when selecting, explaining, and implementing a treatment plan.

Knowing that certain perspectives are the starting points for one or more people who may be involved in treatment lets you know that extra care will need to be taken and specific evidence will need to be presented that points to another explanation. It will also be important to further explore what "lazy" means to this person. She may mean that sometimes the child can do that task and other times he can't, which provides useful information about the child and further avenues to explore. Or this individual, perhaps the classroom teacher, may be annoyed with students who object to doing work she has assigned, suggesting she may need more support in her work with the child, again indicating further avenues to explore. It is critical to ensure that someone holding such a perspective is given the resources to be able to shift his or her view of the child in order to effectively implement a plan.

Step 4: Review Research

This step involves considering all forms of evidence discussed in the last chapter, including the different forms of research. This is the most complicated step in the process, but when carried out thoroughly, it greatly increases the likelihood of success.

Critically reviewing literature and choosing a treatment approach may sound like a daunting task. You may be familiar with one or more approaches to treating this problem, which is a good place to start. However, it is worth considering other approaches. There are, literally, hundreds of books available and articles that you can access through the Internet, at bookstores, and at academic and some large public libraries, describing different clinical approaches, with more or less research support. But nobody can read everything about every approach. Trying to do so will only lead to frustration and very likely further confusion. However, if you have a few favorite clinical writers who summarize research for clinicians, or researchers who are respected in the field, regarding the problem you are targeting, consider their work and opinions.

Research support for a model that seems to fit the problem you are treating, whether or not you are familiar with it, may be worth exploring further. If you are targeting a major expressive language problem, consider the approaches that focus on speech and language acquisition and expression, but also look at some that include augmentative and alternative communication. If you are first targeting a behavior problem, such as refusing to share toys or pushing classmates during recess, consider approaches that include positive behavioral supports and developing social collaboration skills.

Get Team Input

Be sure to tap a variety of sources. The occupational therapist or speech and language pathologist on the child's treatment team may be knowledgable about research related to students with a similar problem. Or you may have a colleague who has worked with a consultant who is knowledgeable about an approach with which you are less familiar. If you are a consultant, you may want to consult other consultants! You can't master every approach described in every research study, but having even a cursory knowledge of several will be worthwhile as you formulate your treatment plan. For example, knowing that Discrete Trial Training can be helpful in teaching certain specific skills, such as matching and sorting, but that the SCERTS™ Model (Prizant, Wetherby, Rubin, Laurent, & Rydell, 2006) is an effective model for understanding and treating emotional dysregulation will likely influence your intervention plan. If the child has needs in both areas, you may decide to use both approaches. The goal will be to introduce and implement these approaches at the appropriate times and in appropriate ways, ensuring that there will be no incompatibilities. Just as you would check for any possible negative side effects that could result from medication interactions, you will want to do the same when determining which treatments to use.

Literature Reviews

Reviewing relevant research literature can be intimidating in and of itself. Again, you can't possibly read everything, but you can look at some basic facets of the research on treating a specific problem. If you don't have access to current journals, most search engines provide access to summaries you can wade through. If there are articles that are particularly relevant, then you can access them through your library. Colleges, universities, and some organizations, such as the American Psychological Association (APA), provide access to most journals online, sometimes for a fee. You can often find studies in which the subjects are similar to the child you are working with in age, developmental stage, cognitive ability, and/or behavioral functioning. The more similarities the subjects have to your child, the more successful you are likely to be.

Think Like a Scientist

As you do your literature review, you will also want to ask if the particular study was reliable. That is, was it repeated? How many times? And were the results similar? Was it valid? Was the data collected relevant to the behaviors targeted in the experiment—and to those you are trying to treat? Was the experiment reviewed by others with appropriate background and training? If so, did the reviewers have a vested interest in the study's outcome? Research treatment reviews published in widely accepted journals can be especially helpful for getting an initial overview of the range of therapies available to treat the specific problem. However, be wary of conclusions prioritizing research rigor over clinical relevance, or if a study purports to be unbiased but is published by authors from one specific orientation or agency that promotes the orientation of the study findings.

If you don't have access to actual research journal articles, books and online resources summarizing bodies of research literature from a variety of perspectives are available. You are likely to encounter a confusing body of literature, with many conflicting findings and conclusions. However, finding a few studies with treatments both similar to and different from what you already know or might be considering helps treatment planning evolve. If your primary responsibility is developing treatment programs for children with autism but you don't have sufficient background in research to evaluate studies, consider collaborating closely with someone who does. Throughout this process, your "treatment as usual" approaches will be challenged, will grow, and will improve.

Step 5: Design the Treatment Plan

At this stage, most of your work is already done. It's now a matter of organizing what you know. After weighing your options based on all of the previous steps, you have the information you need to design your treatment plan. The plan should describe the individuals who will provide the treatment. They might include you, yourself, and/ or another specialist, family members, teachers, therapists, or other providers of education, care, and services for the child. You can't anticipate every aspect of the treatment plan, but you need to think about and plan for a variety of related issues, such as the amount of time that will be required to complete various phases, any training that will be necessary and how much time that will require, who will provide it, and where the treatment will take place. The plan should also include some long- and short-term goals and a realistic timeline for reaching those goals, as well as when and how progress will be evaluated and reevaluated.

All of these steps are necessary so that the treatment team can assess how the plan is working and make needed revisions (see following section). Start a plan with an open mind and evaluate that plan's potential impact, considering at this point that you may need to revise or even scrap it completely. While the latter is unlikely, being receptive to change increases the likelihood of arriving at a maximally successful plan. And, be sure that all members of the treatment team agree on what "successful" means.

Determining Length of Treatment

In some cases, it can take many weeks or even months to determine if the plan is having a positive impact on some kinds of challenges, such as a change in problem behavior. Some problems do get worse before they get better (the "extinction burst" phenomenon), but in general, close monitoring of all aspects of the impact of the plan should be intrinsic to the plan itself. Benchmarks should be built into the plan. For example, if you are working on a feeding issue and trying to increase the number and types of food an underweight child with a very limited repertoire will eat, it will be helpful to come up with a timeline and short-term goals based on medical health, collaborating with the child's pediatrician and also, ideally, a nutritionist and feeding specialist: "The child will eat sufficiently to gain x amount of weight by Week 3" and "The child will eat one formerly refused food from a needed food group by Week 3." A longer-term goal might be: "The child will gain x pounds by Week 12," with weight gain and food choices based on pediatrician and nutritionist input.

Step 6: Evaluate Effectiveness and Generate Your Own Evidence

Once you have developed a plan and have a reasonable expectation that it will be successful, you will need to build in a system for recording data and monitoring progress. Both quantitative and qualitative data are relevant. It is especially important to monitor progress regarding the specific problem you are trying to treat, but also pay attention to the factors you suspect are related to this problem. If your initial treatment isn't successful (i.e., if you have not achieved the goals stated in your treatment plan), then you will have evidence to review and will be more able to reformulate a new hypothesis and treatment plan. For example, one goal may have been to "eliminate yelling during Circle Time." If the child has stopped yelling out during Circle Time in the morning but continues to yell at the Good-bye Circle in the afternoon, you will want to determine what about afternoon Circle is eliciting that behavior, and you may need to treat it in a different way. Looking closely at the conditions, especially the antecedents and setting events, during Morning Circle and comparing them to the Good-bye Circle will help you begin to formulate a new plan. Perhaps the Morning Circle includes more singing, which the child enjoys, whereas the Good-bye Circle has more verbal discussion, which the child cannot access, or perhaps the parents picking kids up is distracting to the child during the Good-bye Circle.

Monitoring Satisfaction

You will also want to monitor "collateral damage" or "collateral gains." That is, you may find that a behavior plan to reduce aggression is successful at eliminating hitting and kicking but has caused a marked increase in negative self-statements, a new problem that will need to be addressed. Or maybe the plan has eliminated aggression and also increased positive social interactions with peers. Both of these collateral impacts will be key to incorporate in the next stage of treatment planning.

Monitoring child and caregiver/adult satisfaction is also part of evaluating success. For example, a child may now be sitting quietly at Morning Meeting and even imitates the hand motions to some of the songs, but he only occasionally makes eye contact with his teacher and peers and rarely smiles. He has achieved his behavioral goals, but lack of positive or socially shared affect is a new concern to address.

In another situation, a 4-year-old spent most of his two hours per day of home-based services crying and refusing to participate in tabletop activities with his home trainer. After five weeks of programming with only minimal progress (he began to sit for two minutes at a time but cried the entire time), his mother chose not to continue. She was experiencing a great deal of stress, and despite her initial support of the program, she convened his team to re-evaluate whether this was the right approach for her child. Together they came up with a new plan that included more physical activity and social games, including hiding and finding objects and playing chase, but worked toward the same goals—and ultimately achieved them.

Evaluating Effectiveness

How does one evaluate the impact of the treatment and actual progress? There are probably as many different ways of doing this as there are models and plans. Recording progress in a way that is manageable to those involved in treatment and that doesn't detract from needed time with the child are generally bottom-line criteria. Using data forms that match how people think about their work with the child and are intuitive greatly increases the likelihood of effective use. Enlisting the assistance of a consultant who is able to observe the child across settings and collect data can also be helpful.

When possible and with appropriate family and programmatic permissions and privacy safeguarding, videotaping a child at home or in the environment in which particular behaviors occur can be uniquely helpful in capturing treatment responses and changes in the child that include both what one has set out to measure as well as those collateral changes. Furthermore, looking at, discussing, and analyzing a video as a team often leads to further hypothesis refinement, improved understanding of the behavior in a natural context, and possibly revised treatment planning.

Help With Data Collection

Qualitative data can be collected through videos, note taking, and interviews, and quantitative components of these can be assimilated. Quantitative data can be collected through paper and pencil means, through the use of graphs, charts, and checklists, or with the computerized forms and relatively user-friendly database programs *in vivo* and/or from video clips.

There is an increasing number of ready-made electronic means for both treatment planning and data collection, and these will become even more available and accessible as technology continues to advance. There are also many web-based data treatment planning and data collection programs, some of which are tied to specific treatment models. Several electronic program planning and data collection systems for Discrete Trial Training programs are currently available, perhaps because the prescriptive nature of this model lends itself readily to a database of this sort. There are also other model-based treatment planning and data collection programs available, although they may be far too expensive for individual purchase. For instance, Relationship Development Intervention (Gutstein & Sheely, 2002) has an extensive operating system, the Dynamic Consultation Tool, which involves, in part, provider creation and family participation in a progress tracking and program planning database built around the RDI curriculum. Autism Pro Professional is another comprehensive web-based treatment planning and data system, which also incorporates staff training in multiple models (http://www.autismpro.com/products/intervention-planning).

Although these systems involve web-based subscriptions, which have advantages and disadvantages but generally require a considerable investment, some data collection systems are more affordable and designed for full individualization, or one can use the curriculum and progress tracking system included in the package. For instance, eCove (eCove Software LLC, Tenny) is constructed such that one can enter any measurable goal (e.g., number of socially directed smiles during a play session; duration of peer interaction in the cafeteria; affect during math class) and readily collect data on it by clicking on a computer, iPad, or various types of smartphones. Not all families or school districts have access to this level of technology, but such products are becoming increasingly affordable and universal. This is only a small sampling of what was available at the time this book was written. No doubt there are dozens of new products and applications, new websites, and ready-made forms that you can download and duplicate.

Step 7: Redesign the Plan as Needed

Now that you have planned, implemented, and collected data on one or more behaviors and evaluated the initial effectiveness of the program, you will want to decide what to do next. This is the important step in which you examine the evidence your treatment process has produced and adjust accordingly. You now have what is generally called "practice-based evidence," which is an extremely important form of evidence since it is specific to the child, problem, and treatment with which you are working. If the intervention was successful, will you need to continue monitoring progress? How and for how long? Will the child need support and instruction in generalizing learned skills?

You will need to make a follow-up plan, including how and where generalization will be taught: This can be relatively straightforward, such as teaching a child to transfer newly learned table manners in another setting (e.g., from school to home or from home to Grandma's house). Or it can be one of the most complex and time-consuming steps of the entire process, such as teaching how to initiate and sustain interactions with peers, first in the classroom, then on the playground, in the cafeteria, at Girl Scouts, or in another environment. Such a plan will take considerable time and effort, but it will likely be successful if the data is analyzed in a comprehensive manner and you are able to re-create or at least draw upon the conditions that led to the child's initial success.

It is likely that other problems need to be addressed. You may want to take a similar approach or consider different or additional treatment. If the intervention isn't helping, or isn't helping as much or as fast as you had expected, you will need to modify the existing treatment, add another treatment, or change approaches entirely in order to solve the same, a related, or perhaps a different problem that has different underlying causes and consequences. Making these decisions in an orderly and organized fashion and doing a careful analysis of each behavior will lead to faster and ultimately more effective treatments.

Unintended Consequences

Sometimes solving one problem can lead to another. For example, a 30-month-old with a PDD-NOS diagnosis didn't have any spoken language and began an intensive home-based program and center-based playgroup. Within a few months he began making some communicative sounds, got some word approximations, and eventually spoke several words. He also became a good imitator. His parents were excited by his rapid progress, but unfortunately the words he chose to imitate were often of the four-letter variety—and he said them loud and clear—in the grocery store, in his doctor's waiting room, at large family gatherings, and in church.

In another case, teaching a very passive preschooler how to request things at school, such as crayons, glue, and blocks, led to his asking for everything, everywhere, and from everyone. He couldn't understand why his requests weren't met with the same enthusiasm or compliance when he asked a stranger for his hat or politely said "my juice" to a sales clerk with regard to some crystal champagne flutes at a department store bridal registry. So, as previously mentioned, the next steps in a plan that has been successful are often related to generalization and discrimination.

Furthermore, once you have achieved success with one problem, such as finding a teaching approach that resulted in the child quickly aquiring more language or eliminated bolting behavior, or the child is no longer withdrawn but now happily engaged, you can then work on the next layer of challenge. This is the onion skin approach to treatment planning: Peel back the initial challenge and then tackle the next layer, informed by what you have learned.

Plan for Changes Over Time

Some challenges need to be addressed in different ways over time, as the child develops, the context changes, or the demands change. An approach that was effective for teaching a 3-year-old to use single words to request food or a toy may no longer help that same child learn how to have conversations when he is 6 years old. The preschooler whose peers clapped for him (part of his positive reinforcement program) every time he asked to use the bathroom needs to learn that first graders do not do that and are generally more reserved and private. So it is important to constantly reevaluate what you are doing and determine if it is still the appropriate treatment plan and you are still trying to achieve the same results. Even if you are successful, you will want to be sure that the goals and the means for getting there are still appropriate to the child's context/environment and developmental level.

Moving From Theory to Practice

Now that you have the basics of this seven-step process, you will want to learn how to put it into practice—at work, in the classroom or clinic, at home, or in the community. The following nine chapters describe cases in which this model has been used in different ways. Each chapter includes a case study that will detail situations that went smoothly from the beginning, as well as some that didn't. The children discussed have some similarities; most notably, they were all given a diagnosis of an autism spectrum disorder at some point, and some still carry that diagnosis. But they vary either in age, developmental stage, school and family circumstances, learning and/or social-emotional profile, or some combination of those elements. They are drawn from real experiences with real children and adolescents, although names and any other identifying characteristics have been changed, and the cases reflect composites across different children.

The problems and solutions described in these cases were chosen, not only because they represent situations that we encounter repeatedly in the population of children that we see in our practices, but also because solving them has enhanced many aspects of life for the child and family and has expanded their world. These have included greater success in academic learning, improved language and social communication, more adaptive and socially acceptable behaviors, reduced anxiety and feelings of isolation, and greater access to community resources, supports, services, and leisure activities. Helping families and treatment teams think about, tackle, and solve some of the problems they face has also provided a way for each child to not only participate more in school and home life but also to contribute their unique gifts and talents in a way they couldn't before.

CHAPTER 4

JAMAL: A PREVIOUSLY HAPPY PRESCHOOLER DISENGAGES

"Jamal is making progress in preschool. He is following directions and learning new skills. But he just doesn't seem as happy as he used to be."

—Jamal's mother

Step 1: Gather Background Information

Jamal is a 3½-year-old boy and the older of two children of Karim and Robin, who have always been very involved with his therapies and education. He had intensive early intervention services and then began attending a specialized preschool for children with autism and related disorders at age 3.

Jamal entered the class just after his third birthday, in accordance with the laws of the state. His initial assessments in speech, occupational therapy, and academic ability, while consistent with his diagnosis of autism, indicated he had strong skills overall. He tested above age level for vocabulary, both expressive and receptive. He displayed beginning pretend play skills; he had a good early number sense; and he could already read some simple words, including a few animals (pig, cow, dog) and some colors (red, blue, green).

Jamal had little difficulty separating from his parents, and he learned the preschool routine quickly, showing independence in many areas after just a few days. He went to his mat on the floor upon request, and he quickly put away his toys when his teacher sang the clean-up song. He was able to find his name at the snack table and pointed to the calendar dates when he was the leader for the morning routine. He exhibited no behavior problems, and his teachers felt he made a good adjustment to the program.

Program Components

The town had developed this full-day, five-day program with extensive expert consultation. The program integrated principles of ABA, often used in preschools, within a traditional preschool curriculum. The day began with a morning meeting, including greetings, sharing news from home and choosing songs, followed by a group story time and choice time with an emphasis on pretend play.

Unlike a more traditional public preschool, the class was smaller (10 students rather than 16 to 18, which is more typical in this state); each activity was broken down into individual steps to enhance learning; visuals accompanied each activity; and the staff:child ratio was 1:2. Children were taught individually using Discrete Trial Training (DTT), and other ABA techniques were used during group times, including use of extensive prompts and a token system. Parents sent in notes so staff could prompt the children during sharing news time, and prompt fading (beginning with maximum prompting and gradually fading support) was used throughout the day.

Two children at a time played at each pretend play center, facilitated by a teacher or aide, who used a combination of scripts for talking suggestions (e.g., "I want to order an ice cream cone") and a picture menu of a variety of items to order. Concrete props were used as staff prompted the children through each step of buying an ice cream cone and getting a haircut, two activities familiar to most children. The staff tracked progress in academic and expressive and receptive language as well as areas of individual need, such as behavior issues or self-help skills. Most children were active participants in the curriculum and made steady progress. Staff and parents were pleased, and the program seemed to be a success.

Step 2: Identify the Problem

Then Karim and Robin began to have concerns about Jamal. They thought he began to "tune out" and was becoming harder to play with than usual after pickup and for the rest of the afternoon after school. He was less responsive to them and to his younger sister, with whom he used to enjoy playing chase and jumping around. They thought this was simply because he was exhausted after a long day at school, but when this pattern persisted beyond the first two months of school, their level of concern increased.

Seeking Out an Experienced Consultant

They raised the issue with the staff, who hadn't picked up any problems, but they had only recently met Jamal and were not aware of his greater range of affect and especially how cheerful he had been in the past. They agreed to have one of their program consultants in to observe.

Nicole, who was an experienced consultant and a BCBA, also had a background in early childhood education and had worked as a preschool teacher for several years. She had helped design the program and thought well of it. However, she recognized that different children have different needs, and although she didn't know Jamal well either, she took the family's concerns seriously.

After interviewing Karim, Robin, and the classroom staff, it was still unclear what the problem was—or even if there was a problem. She then observed Jamal, first at home after school and then at school. She found that he was difficult to engage, lay around much of the time, and responded only with a great deal of prompting from the adults in both settings. She didn't know if this was simply how his autism manifested, as his presentation was similar to many children she had seen. She listened carefully to Karim and Robin, who reported that he used to be much more playful. Upon further questioning, she was able to discern specifically that he used to smile more, romp around with his sister, make more spontaneous verbal comments, frequently brought books to his parents, and enjoyed being read to. They also shared a video that Jamal's Early Intervention providers made when they worked with him at home before he began preschool, and of him at a family birthday party playing with his sister around the same time.

Nicole saw a very different child. In that video he was smiling and referencing a great deal, responded frequently without prompts to the adults' questions, and often made comments while playing. He appeared much more responsive, made frequent eye contact and bids for more play, especially during rough-and-tumble play, but also during silly, pretend routines. In one clip the Early Intervention provider pretended that a Barney doll didn't want his hair cut, just as he, Jamal, didn't want his hair cut, and she imitated his playfully emphatic "NO WAY!" a phrase Jamal often used when he didn't want to do something, as he laughed and looked at the provider. Nicole too felt he appeared much more energetic, happier, and more engaged.

Nicole then observed at school. Jamal followed the class routine flawlessly, as the staff had indicated. However, he appeared very different than on the video. He rarely smiled. He only initiated interactions to request help in getting his coat on and off. He responded to staff prompts but did not expand or extend the play. He looked away during the small group instruction unless he was called on, and he appeared to be talking to himself much of the time. He didn't respond to peers when they approached him. He appeared quite similar at home and at school but very different on the Early Intervention video and also in contrast to his parents' description of his past behavior.

Looking for Explanations

Since beginning preschool, Jamal's affect had become flat and he appeared underaroused both at school and home. There was a sharp contrast between his presentation on the video in the past and how he presented now. Nicole felt it would be helpful to "unpack" or operationalize the problem more specifically. In the video clips he engaged in much more of the following behaviors:

> Social smiling with eye contact
> Initiation in various ways—verbal, gestures, with toys
> Spontaneous requests for an adult to continue to play
> Much more use of socially directed language
> Much less talking to himself

So she narrowed the questions down:

- Why does Jamal appear so much more engaged, as defined by these behaviors, in his Early Intervention sessions and by parent description, at home, than he does now at home and at school?
- For whom is this a problem and how is it affecting them?

This problem was of great concern to Jamal's parents, who saw a dramatic difference. His school team had at first thought his parents were "in denial" about how he behaved at home and felt he really was doing well at school—until they viewed the video. Then all agreed that this was an important problem to address. All of the adults felt that Jamal's social language and learning were being limited by his underarousal and lack of interest or participation at school.

Step 3: State the Hypothesis, Yours and Others'

Possibly Jamal had some sort of global regression. Although regressions at around 6 months (Zwaigenbaum et al., 2005) and 15 to 18 months (Werner and Dawson, 2005) have been documented in multiple research studies, it is unusual for children as old as 3 to regress. However, it is always important to first rule out a medical cause in such circumstances. His parents reported that he had had a few ear infections since starting school, but he also had had a history of ear infections every winter. Otherwise he had been healthy.

Just to be absolutely certain, Nicole suggested they take him to his pediatrician, who referred him to a developmental pediatrician to look for any possible explanations for the set of changes Nicole and his family had identified, and no medical issues surfaced. The developmental pediatrician asked Jamal's parents if there were times when he was "his old self." It turned out his parents had hired his old Early Intervention provider to work with him every other Saturday, and during these sessions he did seem more like his old self. While this didn't rule out a medical contribution to what appeared to be a regression, it suggested the answer could be related more to the differences in approach and style of the EI provider compared to the preschool staff, or a difference in the dynamics of group activities versus one-on-one activities, or both.

She briefly wondered, "Could the school program be too difficult for him to access in some way? Was the academic content too challenging?" But she quickly dismissed any problem with the cognitive load; Jamal was bright and the activities in the video were similar to those in the class. Was the delivery of instruction at school (e.g., language pace) too fast? She knew that sometimes, even when the content is accessible to children, the pace is too fast to process, so they learn to tune out. However, the pacing in the video of the adult language and of the play was similar to that in school, maybe even a little faster. Was waiting for others to respond creating too much downtime, making it difficult for Jamal to stay involved in activities at school?

This could be a contributing factor. However, he tuned out even during adult-facilitated pretend play with two children and a pretend script, and also during his one-on-one speech therapy. Had she not observed him during one-on-one sessions, this would have been a critical next step, since there was a major difference between Early Intervention and preschool. The high ratios and amount of dyad and one-on-one times within this program made this a less likely hypothesis.

Was Jamal overwhelmed by the size of the preschool class? He was showing the same lack of engagement during his one-on-one times outside of school, suggesting this wasn't the case, but perhaps he had difficulty becoming engaged quickly while in a large group at school. She continued with this line of questioning: Could there be subtle differences between the styles and approaches of the Early Intervention provider and his current school staff?

Same Techniques, Different Styles

Nicole analyzed the video again in an effort to find differences. The Early Intervention provider was a paraprofessional who was supervised by a BCBA using techniques that "on paper" were the same as at school. In studying the video, however, she noticed that the EI provider smiled much more throughout her session in such a way that somehow got Jamal to smile back. They had many slowly paced, back-and-forth playful interactions in between the more demanding work tasks. She also reinforced each of Jamal's initiations by immediately responding with something related to what he did or said, even when this meant veering from the program she was teaching. For example, in one clip they were working on labeling pictures and Jamal suddenly got up from the table, got a cup from the breakfast nook, and gave it to her. The provider commented, "Oh, you got that CUP that matches the picture!" pretending to drink from it while making silly gulping sounds. Jamal smiled at her in response, reached for the cup, then also pretended to drink and gulp.

Nicole noticed that the EI provider was very repetitive at the beginning of each activity, and that Jamal would begin the activity in the serious, quiet state he was in at school, but after a few repetitions both would be smiling. Then the provider would add complexity. She was creating a subtle "dance" by increasing emotional enjoyment and then increasing participation by Jamal. She then compared this to her observations at school. Jamal's teachers were using very similar approaches, yet she noted that most of the school staff did not respond to Jamal's initiations if they were not in direct response to the specific task. She also noticed that while they smiled as they praised him, they worked with him in a studious, serious way most of the time. Nicole's working hypothesis began to take shape: Although EI and the school staff were implementing ABA techniques and engaging in similar activities, they had very different styles and elicited very different responses.

Step 4: Review Treatment Approaches

Nicole then decided to review the research on several topics she thought were most relevant to her questions. These included studies on approaches to helping children attain a positive and engaged emotional state, including increasing the behaviors that had occurred more frequently in the past and now were occurring less frequently.

She first did a Google search on "autism treatments and affect," hoping to find research on techniques that helped children with autism show more positive, socially directed affect. She waded through research articles on teaching children with ASD about emotions and on parent emotions before finding some studies related more directly to approaches for increasing positive child emotion. She reviewed some studies on Pivotal Response Training and on Floortime™ and positive emotion in children. She read up on Floortime™ and thought that even though the Early Intervention provider was using an ABA approach, her use of her own emotions in initiating and responding, which seemed to stimulate Jamal's emotional connections to her, sounded like the descriptions in the Floortime™ book she skimmed (Greenspan & Wieder, 2006). She also found several articles on PRT, including "Improving Social Initiations in Young Children with Autism Using Reinforcers with Embedded Social Interactions" (Koegel, Vernon, & Koegel, 2009), and she read about the Early Start Denver Model (Rogers & Dawson, 2009) and noted their emphasis on the adult creating a positive emotional experience for the child during instruction as part of their "fidelity measure." She came upon a quote in a published interview by Sally Rogers, in which she talked about "finding the smiles" as key to teaching (Parker-Pope, 2009) and thought of Jamal's serious face now and his social smiles in the video in the past.

Nicole considered her observations and impressions, both of Jamal and the provider in the video, especially the difference in his emotional expressions and how the provider got him involved in activities, as well as the literature she had found regarding adult use of positive emotion, both from the behavioral and the developmental and relational literature. She also considered parent reports about the differences they noted.

Time to Warm Up

During her school observations, the teachers were implementing all of the procedures she and her consultation team had recommended. Although most of the children were responding, they weren't doing much smiling at or with Jamal, and they weren't "warming him up" with an easy, repetitive startup of tasks that was so apparent in the video. This process appeared to help him get into a happy and more interactive state, which was also referred to in the behavioral literature ("behavioral momentum"), the Floortime™ literature, and the ESDM. The other children in Jamal's class, all of whom were a bit more advanced, seemed to not need this preparation, but perhaps Jamal did.

Nicole also looked at some literature on arousal, as Jamal appeared underaroused and his affect appeared flat. His occupational therapist at school reported that in her sessions, he seemed much more like the Jamal in the EI video and suggested incorporating more gross and fine motor activity into Jamal's day. The OT designed a "sensory diet," which is a carefully planned schedule of motor and sensory activities designed to increase attention, alertness, and emotional regulation throughout the day. Nicole came across a concept article describing a "Social Affective Diet" (Levine, Chedd, & Bauch, 2009) and thought this approach too might be helpful to Jamal's team in creating a plan. This is a term the authors coined to represent the overt effort to infuse positive interactive experiences into a child's day in order to get him into a happy, socially interactive state.

More Than One Approach Needed

Although every member of the team had different training and experience, as well as their own preferred approaches, they agreed on one thing, that one approach was not going to work for Jamal and that he needed elements of several in order to achieve the goal of becoming more happily engaged and involved in learning, playing, and socializing.

Step 5: Designing the Treatment Plan

So with no clear-cut answers, but some hypotheses supported by clinical judgment and informed by careful observations and information gathering about Jamal, as well as her review of some of the most relevant literature, Nicole met with Jamal's school and family team. She showed them all of the videos and shared her recommendation to create more social engagement and playful interactions, especially as a warm-up activity before starting the regular preschool curriculum. No trained Floortime™ professionals were available in the area, so the team reviewed some materials online about this approach. One teacher had recently attended a workshop on Floortime™, and while she was by no means an expert, she reported what she learned and shared her handouts, including some about the roles of emotions in teaching and some suggested activities to help children make emotional connections.

Targeting Behaviors for Data Collection

The team then chose some specific behaviors to measure to determine if they were having an impact. Although they wanted to track Jamal's progress all day, they decided to initially target affect and behavior during pretend play and individual therapy sessions, as these were the times when he had individual support and instruction. It would be easiest both to teach and implement a different teaching style and to collect data during those times. They decided to collect data on a few key differences in Jamal's behavior between the EI video and school, discussing and writing descriptions of three specific behaviors. They planned to record data during four 5-minute intervals of activity, as the pretend play and therapy sessions ran about 30 minutes. They also got parental permission to film him during these activities, as the Team could see the contrast between EI and school and felt that observing this new approach, if it worked, would also be apparent.

The team used the following:

Data Collection Form

ACTIVITY	1	2	3	4
Socially directed smiles				
Socially directed relevant unprompted language				
Unprompted continued participation in activity				

Some staff felt comfortable trying this new approach, but others reported feeling awkward and less confident, as they hadn't had formal training. However, they all agreed that there was no apparent risk of harm. If they did not see a strong response in Jamal, they would look into hiring another consultant with expertise in one of the autism treatment models in which increasing social–emotional connections is a key component (e.g., Floortime™, ESDM, PRT).

So the initial plan included first taking baseline data for a week. Jamal's classroom staff and therapists would be responsible for recording data, both before and after studying and practicing the EI provider's playful style and repetition of routines to start the activities. Data would be collected for two weeks (an AB design).

Step 6: Evaluate Effectiveness and Generate Your Own Evidence

In tracking and recording Jamal's progress, they found that in the second 10 minutes of time, all three items showed dramatic increase.

Baseline before making changes:

Speech Therapy	1	2	3	4
Socially directed smiles	0	0	1	0
Socially directed relevant unprompted language	0	0	0	0
Unprompted continued participation in activity	0	1	1	0

After making the changes in adult style in therapies and pretend play:

Speech Therapy	1	2	3	4
Socially directed smiles	4	6	2	0
Socially directed relevant unprompted language	3	5	3	0
Unprompted continued participation in activity	3	6	4	0

In evaluating the data across situations and staff, it seemed the changes in staff style and affect led to a dramatic increase in Jamal's social participation and smiles at first, but then decreased. The school team was pleased with the changes and wanted more training in incorporating this method into the rest of Jamal's school day. A Floortime™ specialist was eventually located, who first observed Jamal and the classroom routine and then conducted an initial in-service training. Staff did not learn all about Floortime™ in this limited amount of time, but because the consultation was very targeted to their classroom and Jamal's needs specifically, they did learn several strategies to try.

Step 7: Redesign the Plan as Needed

The team continued to take data over the next month. Karim and Robin would continue to engage in emotionally engaging, highly motivating social play with Jamal at home, and although they couldn't commit to taking data formally, they would try to keep tabs and make notes on his affect and engagement. If there was no regression in either setting, the team would taper down to taking data sporadically, but at least twice per month. If school and family did not feel sufficient progress was being made, the team agreed to increase consultation time from the Floortime™ specialist, as well as continue to keep up with the research on increasing positive affect and engagement in children with autism spectrum disorders.

CHAPTER 5

KATHERINE:
A 9-YEAR-OLD LEARNS TO
COPE WITH HER OWN
EXPLOSIVE EPISODES

"She has so much going for her. She's bright and creative and she wants to be 'one of the gang.' If only she could keep her emotions under control and not go off the deep end when things don't go her way . . ."

Katherine's classroom teacher

Step 1: Gather Background Information

Katherine is a 9-year-old girl who was diagnosed with PDD-NOS at age 2 years 9 months based on her delays in expressive language and, to a lesser extent, receptive language, lack of eye contact and gestural communication, and atypical and repetitive play skills. She didn't play with stuffed animals, dolls, play sets, like the toy kitchen or farm that her grandparents bought her, or even with balls or blocks. She preferred noisy cause-and-effect toys and one particular music video. Since that time, Katherine has become more verbal and interactive, even friendly. However, she continues to have some language processing problems and difficulties with social communication. She has a couple of friends with whom she plays computer fantasy games, and she does well in reading and social studies, but she has a difficult time with math and more complex language arts instruction, especially answering abstract questions about reading assignments.

Katherine got early intervention services for about 10 months before entering preschool. They consisted of a weekly playgroup and two hours at home with a developmental educator and sometimes an occupational therapist. Since then, she has been in an integrated classroom, beginning with a small preschool class that was reportedly "behaviorally based," using some ABA interventions but not exclusively. Then she had a shared aide in first grade who gave her academic support primarily, and she has always gotten school-based speech therapy and occupational therapy, both in the classroom and on a pull-out basis once a week.

Many Services in Place

Her parents feel that all of her services have helped "a little" but nothing has helped "a lot." They put into place an afterschool, six hour per week ABA program, which she has participated in for the past year. This has also helped a little, specifically, helping her choose activities from a visual schedule and complete them without getting angry or frustrated. She thoroughly enjoys playing with her therapist, earning tokens, and then trading them in at the end of the week for special privileges, but she doesn't seem to carry over these skills "in real life," as her parents put it.

Katherine lives with her parents, her two brothers, ages 12 and 14, and her dog in a quiet suburban neighborhood. Katherine's brothers do reasonably well in school, have friends, and participate in various afterschool activities. "They're just normal, easygoing kids. They had none of the problems we've been dealing with," says Katherine's mother.

Step 2: Identify the Problem

Katherine has frequent outbursts and temper tantrums, both at home and at school. Sometimes they happen in her third-grade classroom, when she doesn't understand an assignment or thinks she has "messed up." Other times they occur at gym or recess, during afterschool play and unstructured activities, or during unusual or unscheduled events. These might include a schoolwide assembly, when there is a substitute teacher, or during a recent guest "read-aloud" program, in which the school principal, librarian, and several parents participated. Most of the class enjoyed the break from the usual routine, but Katherine was agitated and seemed extremely uncomfortable. Was it because she just didn't expect it? Her teacher noticed that she was looking unhappy and asked if she wanted to take a break and a walk, which she did. She returned to the class at the very end of the "read-aloud" and missed almost the entire event, including an interactive game based on some of the characters in one of the stories and a special snack. This was unfortunate because she would have enjoyed both.

Unpredictability Causes Anxiety

Katherine's outbursts can get extreme and include loud screaming and long crying spells, although she rarely gets aggressive or hurtful toward her peers or brothers. Her parents and teachers can predict that some situations will set her off, like explaining an unfamiliar, multistep homework assignment, especially in math, or introducing a new game or sports activity. In such cases, they speak slowly, break down instructions into very simple steps, and even illustrate what needs to be done.

However, many other situations that cause outbursts are impossible to predict and some seem so minor. She may explode without warning or run out of the room in tears. This happened on one occasion, when she got to the public library and only three of the five CDs she requested were available. "In a split second, Katherine's face turned crimson," recalled her mother. "She screeched and then bolted out the front door of the library, leaving several startled and worried patrons in her wake." When her parents brought up the episode later that night, she seemed very embarrassed and said, "Be quiet. Don't talk about it."

Katherine had another similar reaction at school the following week. She had been practicing a song with five other girls for the upcoming school play. One of the girls announced at their practice that she wouldn't be able to sing on the first night—she had to go to her grandmother's 75th birthday party—but she would be there the following afternoon and evening for the next two performances. "Katherine absolutely lost it," the drama teacher recalled. "She started screaming and crying. She told the girl that she had to be there, that she couldn't go to her grandmother's party, that it wasn't fair." Then the other girls began to get upset, tear up, and the rest of them began to take sides and argue. "It was a disaster," continued her mother. "Katherine just can't tolerate changes or make exceptions."

Step 3: State the Hypothesis, Yours and Others'

When Katherine is in a predictable situation and/or when she has control over who does what, how, and when, her moods are stable and she appears rational. But when the unexpected occurs, reason goes out the window and her emotions take over. While the adults couldn't always predict what sort of event would set her off, in retrospect it was always clear there was some sort of unexpected, often disappointing element, even a small one. Katherine's parents, her school team, and her outside therapist are seeing the same behaviors and agree that they have to be addressed. They all feel that she has made considerable progress in terms of language and social interactions, in problem solving and organization, and even in academic skills since she was first diagnosed with PDD-NOS. However, emotional regulation continues to elude her.

Is It Autism or Something Else?

Despite her gains, Katherine still may be dealing with some of the defining characteristics of autism, although in a much milder way and to a lesser degree. She can express herself verbally and comprehends spoken language well, but she misses some of the social nuances and nonverbal communication—the gestures, tone of voice, those "looks" that might indicate that others are upset or frustrated with her. She lacks what autism specialist Simon Baron-Cohen and others might call the ability to mind-read (Baron-Cohen & Wheelwright, 2004; Hadwin, Howlin, & Baron-Cohen, 2008).

Katherine's rigidity is also standing in the way of her success. She has a set agenda in her mind. It's great when everything happens as she expects. If not, it's a disaster in her mind. A further complication is that she has no ability to regulate her emotions. When things don't happen according to plan, she cannot cope and becomes extremely sad, angry and loud. She has little ability to self-calm or to make an alternative plan. She doesn't just get upset; she explodes.

Her behaviors have immediate, far-reaching short- and long-term effects on many more people than may be initially apparent. When they occur at school, her outbursts are upsetting to her teachers and disruptive to the students in her class. There may be other ramifications that spread far beyond the classroom walls or the school day. Students talk, gossip, and tend to swap "war stories" during recess and lunch, during other less-structured times, such as at the library or in the cafeteria, and they may also extend their chatter outside, and on the way to and from school.

Problems Affect Everyone in the Family

Sadly, but not surprisingly, Katherine's reactions and upsets are well-known to the entire school community. Katherine's parents know all too well how severe her behaviors are based on their experiences at home. Family meals end abruptly; homework doesn't get done; and her parents end up in long discussions about what they could or should have done, and these discussions can escalate into more intense disagreements about dozens of other topics, some of them totally unrelated. Her mother commented, "Although we recognize this pattern and should know better than to get into the same fights over and over, we all still get sucked into the vortex when Katherine has an outburst."

Further complicating matters, Katherine's parents have heard through the grapevine—their upper-middle-class community is relatively small and families of young children congregate in the same shopping malls and community locales—that Katherine is a real problem at school. Although friends and neighbors usually say the right things ("It must be so hard for you," "I wish I could help"), Katherine's parents feel marginalized and ashamed, as if they have failed as parents. After all, the vast majority of kids in their town appear to be typical, reasonably bright, happy, and well behaved, at least at school. Somehow Katherine's outbursts make her parents feel like it is their fault or even her fault, and they sense others' disapproval, too.

Behaviors Hard to Handle for Friends

Most important, Katherine's inability to cope with unexpected changes, new information, or exceptional circumstances adversely affects her in multiple ways. She has few friends, spends most of her time during lunch and recess alone, and is beginning to dread going to school. When she has meltdowns in class, she is often removed and misses the explanations and opportunities to practice academic work, further feeding the flames of her discomfort. She is aware of how challenging her behaviors can be, at least sometimes, but once an episode occurs and it is over, talking about it just makes it more painful for everyone involved, so Katherine and everyone around her avoid discussion. Her self-esteem has plummeted, and she looks and feels sad and withdrawn most of the time.

Katherine likes having friends and has a few. She wants to continue to get together with them at school and outside of school, but she can see them pulling away from her. She doesn't really know why, but she knows she is different.

To summarize, Katherine's parents and teachers would like to help her:

Not make a mountain out of a molehill (as they put it)
Become more aware of, and then responsive to, the needs and
    feelings of others
Tolerate change and "the unexpected"
Control her severe reactions when things don't go exactly
    as planned and behave in a more socially acceptable way

Step 4: Consider Treatment Approaches and Opinions

While Katherine's parents and school team have brainstormed and discussed a variety of interventions and approaches that may help her, they haven't yet come up with a plan that everyone can agree upon. Her classroom teacher, who isn't formally trained in special education but has taken numerous workshops on inclusion, thought that a more consistent reward system might help. Creating a structure in which Katherine would earn tokens for appropriate behaviors each day but not lose them for inappropriate behaviors, and then exchange them at the end of each week for "prizes," such as nail polish and lip gloss, may be very motivating, she reasoned. She could even save up her tokens and then trade them in for a big-ticket item, like an iTunes gift card.

The team considered other approaches as well. The school psychologist thought that while she might be motivated by such a reward system, she really wouldn't be learning specific replacement skills that she could apply at school, home, in social situations, or anywhere else. "She may be rewarded for one response one day and for another response on another day," the psychologist explained. "She wouldn't necessarily get any more understanding of why she should or shouldn't react in a certain way." The speech and language pathologist agreed and took it one step further, stating: "Even if her behaviors improved, she would also need to learn how to recognize when to use which skills. For example, she can't read facial expressions or gestures very well. She doesn't really know when she is being annoying or inappropriate, and she has to learn these things."

Katherine's occupational therapist weighed in as well. Her opinion was that Katherine needed more sensory input to help her calm down. In fact, a sensory profile that her parents and school team filled out at the beginning of the school year indicated that she had greater sensory needs than most students her age. The OT suggested frequent breaks throughout the day and a "sensory diet" that would include regular opportunities to move around, stretch, manipulate objects of various textures, and engage in other activities that would help her self-calm. The school social worker thought she might need weekly one-on-one sessions, during which she could talk about her feelings and frustrations. The way things stood now, Katherine would meet with her on an as-needed basis, which usually meant when she had already had a big meltdown or did something inappropriate at home and her parents insisted that she "talk to somebody."

No Single Explanation

Katherine's parents were totally confused about the lack of a single coherent explanation for her behavior, but they felt that everybody on the team was making some sense. They did some

research of their own and came across several approaches to dealing with the problems Katherine had been having. They had
heard about Social Stories™ in the past, but their impression was
that they were really only for preschoolers. However, when they
dug deeper into the literature, they decided that these might
help Katherine learn about what to do and what not to do in
social situations—like social "crib sheets." They also found some
information on video modeling, which can involve commercially
packaged video curricula and also taped sessions of individual
students and groups in session, and they thought these might also
help Katherine see herself through others' eyes. Katherine was
already in a social skills group with three other girls once a week.
Although her speech therapist reported that she did well and was
one of the more enthusiastic participants, she didn't seem to be
carrying over skills outside of the group, at least not consistently.
Having actual videos to view repeatedly and being able to access
them when a similar problem arose might help her to both repair
her mistakes and generalize.

Then they came across an interesting website and some articles on an educational, research-based model that addresses the
core deficits of autism: the SCERTS® model (Prizant, Wetherby,
Rubin, Laurent, & Rydell, 2007). The acronym stands for Social
Communication—Emotional Regulation—Transactional Support.
(See Appendix A for a more detailed description.) This, they felt,
was what she and the team really needed, as it included a systematic
way to address all of the deficits that prevented Katherine from being more successful throughout her day, in a variety of situations,
and it was a model that incorporated a variety of techniques, including all of the ones suggested by the team.

They liked the fact that it didn't "forbid" the use of any particular intervention or dictate that procedures be followed in an
exact, rigid way. They also liked the family-centered philosophy
and emphasis on improving family relationships, not only teaching

specific skills. They approached the school team with information about SCERTS®, including several research studies that supported its effectiveness.

At first there was some reluctance, because although some of the team members had heard of SCERTS®, they didn't know much about how to implement it. Some thought it was designed for much younger children; others thought it had only to do with speech and language. Nevertheless, they decided to keep an open mind and find out more.

Need for More Training

The team chair did her own research and discovered that this model was being used in several schools, both public, integrated, and inclusion classrooms, as well as in specialized private schools for students on the autism spectrum. She found out that there were several workshops as well as a three-day intensive training program scheduled, both within a reasonable driving distance from the school. The best news was that the workshops were going to be presented by two of the creators of the model. Longer, more intensive training was available as well.

The team chair decided that she would go to a one-day workshop, as it seemed like a good investment; from what she read, the model might be useful in several classrooms and possibly in other schools within the district. She also offered to foot the bill for Katherine's speech therapist to attend. Katherine's parents decided that it was worth attending too, and they also signed up at their own expense, reasoning that they had spent thousands of dollars over the past decade on books, various play and social groups, and other interventions. Sometimes they worked; sometimes they didn't. Although they were realistic enough to know that there is no "magic bullet," and this wouldn't solve every single problem, they felt that the cost of the workshop was within their budget and sounded like it might provide a good source of ideas and also a way to meet other parents and educators struggling with similar problems.

They attended the one-day workshop and, as often happens, they left with a sense of optimism and a new resolve to put the SCERTS® program into place. However, the team chair felt that more intensive training would be necessary if the team was really going to implement this plan the right way. She met with the team, including Katherine's parents, and gave a presentation on their very limited but informative exposure to learning the SCERTS® approach. She then approached the Director of Student Services, who, understandably, was concerned about the prospect of spending a lot of money. However she liked what she heard about SCERTS®.

The team considered starting the approach using the two comprehensive SCERTS® books, as they had read that this was one way the model could be readily implemented. However, several team members wanted more personalized teaching to learn this model. Because the team chair presented several research studies along with the material from the workshop describing the approach and some short YouTube videos in which one can clearly see SCERTS® in action, the Director of Student Services agreed that further training would be worth the investment.

Make Training Cost Effective

So the plan was to arrange for SCERTS® training, not only for Katherine's team, but also for several other special education teams within the district. However, the training was a couple of months away, and they wanted to put some supports in place right away. The team, including the school's autism specialist, who has some background in ABA and Floortime™, her classroom teacher and the classroom aide, and the occupational therapist, who has some sensory integration training, worked together to design an initial plan.

They realized that they'd been largely reactive in the past. That is, they would wait until Katherine had one of her meltdowns, and then they did something about it. Much of the time they had to respond in the moment, which often involved removing her from a situation and doing "damage control," rather than taking a preventive, skill-building approach. In principle they all decided that the latter would be more beneficial.

The team concluded that they would not dispose of or disregard all that they knew about emotional and behavioral regulation, but that adding SCERTS® to the mix and using it as an organizing framework was sensible.

Step 5: Design the Treatment Plan

First they decided to conduct a full Functional Behavioral Assessment (FBA) in order to identify the triggers (antecedents) of Katherine's behaviors and the consequences. What seemed to cause and what followed Katherine's outbursts? Was some specific condition or event maintaining her behaviors? What was in it for her, if anything?

They also decided that Katherine should meet with the school psychologist weekly instead of only after something went wrong. These sessions could occur during recess, which hadn't been fun for her anyway, and would serve as general check-ins about academic and social issues, and they could address specific problems and strategies for solving them.

Problem-Solving Model

The school psychologist had some training in using Collaborative Problem Solving (Greene & Ablon, 2006). This approach has a strong research base for treating typically developing children, although it was not developed specifically for children who also have a PDD-NOS diagnosis. However, the school psychologist felt that Katherine has sufficient language, cognitive functioning, and social skills to try it. In this approach, Katherine and the involved adults would work together to help Katherine identify what, specifically, in the situations she often found herself in, presented a problem for her (e.g., confusing classwork) and identify her reason for becoming upset about the work—that she didn't understand it and she wouldn't be able to do it right; and recognize the teacher's need to teach the work and to have a way to assess her understanding. Together they would come up with solutions to try. For example, Katherine might suggest having someone explain each step, focusing on one problem at a time, or doing easier work first or having more time to complete work or maybe all of these. Then she and her teacher could work toward a common solution that would take into account both of their needs.

The school psychologist was also experienced with Cognitive Behavior Therapy (CBT) and felt that while this is an effective treatment for anxiety, some components of this would be useful for Katherine, especially teaching her how to use positive self-talk to perhaps reduce her tendency to "catastrophize." Katherine often used many negative phrases about herself when she became distressed, such as screaming at her friends when they announced that they couldn't come to play rehearsal: "Now the whole play will be terrible and everybody will laugh at me and think I'm terrible."

Katherine would continue attending her weekly social group, but the focus would change somewhat. The guidance counselor and speech therapist would co-lead the group and also work on difficult social situations and some ways to handle different types of conversations. They would do this through role-playing and also experiment with video modeling, as she had recently read a summary article that looked at several studies (Bellini & Akullian, 2007), and it appeared to be quite effective for problems like Katherine's.

Prevention Trumps Intervention

Katherine would also continue to get some support in the classroom, including previewing some of the academic work that had been challenging for her and carrying over the solutions she learned through use of the CPS approach. In addition, the classroom aide would also monitor her affect and any breakdowns in communication so she could take a more preventive role and intervene before Katherine escalated and exploded.

Katherine's aide agreed to monitor the social dynamics on the playground and, similarly, she would assist before a situation became problematic. She consulted with the school psychologist, speech therapist, and autism specialist so she would have a better idea of what to look for and what to do before a social encounter became "too hot to handle," and Katherine and her peers would simply have to be split up or were sent off in different directions to timeouts, which had never really worked in the past.

Although the team admitted that their plan included a variety of different methods and strategies, all of the approaches were compatible and worked with, rather than against, each other. They looked at this issue very closely and concluded that Katherine would be getting consistent, rather than mixed, messages, primarily focused on preventive strategies and problem solving. Each of the methods they discussed could be added to her and the team's "bag of tricks," and each of the approaches involved Katherine's having a key role in her own treatment, which the team felt was a useful direction to take. Their biggest challenge would be teaching her how and when to use her new strategies.

Katherine's team decided to closely monitor any changes in behavior during the following two months and then reevaluate. But whatever the results, they committed to attending the three-day SCERTS® workshop, because they all agreed that it would create a useful structure to work with across home and school, for

Katherine and the whole school ultimately, and one in which any successful strategies they had developed by then could readily be incorporated.

Step 6: Evaluate Effectiveness and Generate Your Own Evidence

The result of the FBA confirmed what they all suspected, that Katherine's outbursts occurred when the unexpected happened, when things didn't go her way, and when she misunderstood instructions or interpreted someone's comments as hurtful, although they may not have been intended that way. The consequences of Katherine's behavior were almost always that she would leave or be removed from the situation. So it may have been "escape" that was maintaining her behaviors. Seeking escape may have also been the only way she knew to cope with intense angry, sad emotions. Yet escape was also decreasing her potential to access her peers or to develop more adaptive skills for responding to challenging situations, and so was not resulting in a long term productive solution for her.

The team discussed this and felt that because subsequently she wouldn't get what she wanted, escape was the best tool she had for coping, but it wasn't really what was reinforcing to her. That is, she may have escaped a situation she couldn't tolerate, but she had no appropriate means to communicate her needs, negotiate a solution, or regulate her responses. They didn't think forcing her to stay in an uncomfortable or conflictual setting, for instance, would reduce the behaviors. These issues were discussed, and working with her to develop new, flexible, more adaptive coping skills became the number-one focus of the entire team.

Student Input Increases Likelihood of Success

Katherine liked having a say in her plan. She came up with an idea that her teacher and aide supported: She would raise her hand with a pointer finger up as a sign to the teacher or aide to indicate she was beginning to feel confused. Then one of them would know to come help her right away, and she would not get upset, yell, or "ruin the whole class," as she put it.

The FBA process also established a baseline of frequency, intensity, and duration of Katherine's outbursts across different settings, and Katherine and her team continued to work out situation-specific solutions. What worked in her quiet classroom didn't necessarily work on the noisy playground. This was very helpful in monitoring progress of the treatments overall.

Additional Interventions Also Yield Positive Results

Katherine enjoyed meeting regularly with the school psychologist and gradually became more able to talk about her frustrations and anger, to practice tolerating small frustrations with a supportive adult in a safe setting, and to come up with mutually workable solutions that she could use in the classroom with both academic and social difficulties. Also helpful was learning positive self-talk. She and the psychologist created a mantra for Katherine to repeat to herself (or even out loud) when she got agitated: "I'll do it, but I DON'T have to like it," which she thought was very funny. The girls in her social group joined in, too, and the entire group could often be heard saying in unison, when homework was assigned on a weekend, for example, "We'll do it, but we DON'T have to like it!"

Visual Aids Enhance Learning

Katherine also learned some social rules and norms through watching some social skills video programs, as well as filming some of her own social skills sessions. At first, it was difficult for her to understand what she was doing "wrong," and she continued to insist that everything had to go her way—like when she wanted to play UNO, but the three other girls present wanted to play "GO FISH." However, by going over and over the videos and looking at and discussing the looks on her classmates' faces and their other body language and listening to what they were saying, she slowly began to become more flexible. Compromising and not calling all the shots in similar circumstances continue to be very challenging for her, and it is a topic she is working on through CPS and lots of practice.

Developing Self-Awareness

Working with her school psychologist and outside therapist, Katherine also learned to become more aware of the situations that might upset her, and so she has been more able to ask for breaks, take deep breaths, use her positive self-talk, and begin to generate solutions to situations before they go awry, using new CPS and other strategies. Her teacher and aide have become more involved and have supported all of her attempts to strategize in challenging situations. Although it doesn't work every time—she still gets upset and occasionally yells—she has stopped running out of the classroom. Instead she sits at her desk and says, sometimes out loud, "I'm just going to be angry for a while," which is preferable to bolting and disrupting the entire class. Impressively, the frequency, intensity, and duration data all dropped quite dramatically. Although Katherine's parents and teachers sensed she was doing better, it was helpful to look at this data in black and white and see the actual numbers. It became clear based on the collected data that some situations no longer were associated with upsets (e.g., academic instruction), whereas other situations continued to result in some outbursts (recess and other unstructured social situations). Hence they decided to put more support into recess time.

Parent Support a Helpful Addition

Finally, Katherine's parents, who were at first reluctant to talk about her challenges to other parents or to her peers, decided to "come out of the closet." They went to a class meeting that included presentations on a variety of topics related to inclusion, and they talked briefly about the things that were difficult for Katherine and how her classmates could be supportive. They also told the parents in attendance how fortunate they felt to have Katherine in her local school, along with the kids in her neighborhood, and that she was learning a great deal and they could see her progress "almost daily." This, too, made a tremendous difference, not necessarily in changing Katherine's behaviors, but in reducing the stress that the whole family was feeling. Interestingly, several parents approached them, either after the meeting or on subsequent occasions when they ran into each other at the local mall, and shared their own stories about brothers or sisters or other relatives who had a wide variety of special needs, some similar to Katherine's.

More Frequent Meetings

Katherine's school team decided to meet with her parents monthly, rather than quarterly, as they had been doing previously. They felt that keeping track of her progress and adding to their own evidence base about what was or wasn't working would lead to more rapid change and progress as well as perhaps prevent small annoyances from mushrooming into huge problems. They also decided to convene the team for a half-day session after the SCERTS® training so that all team members could benefit. The parents and school team were excited to learn about a workshop in the area on the Collaborative Problem Solving approach, which they felt was also contributing to Katherine's progress, They felt learning more about using this approach could be helpful for working with Katherine at home and at school, as well as with many other students throughout the district, and would fit in well with the SCERTS® model.

CHAPTER 6

BRANDON: DEVELOPMENTAL DELAYS AND OCD PRESENT A BIG CHALLENGE FOR A NONVERBAL PRESCHOOLER

"He had been doing so well, we thought we completely understood him. Then it all seemed to fall apart. After we reworked his program and he was thriving again, we are feeling relieved and proud! We especially enjoy that he is now asking his peers to play chase with him at recess!"

—Brandon's classroom teacher

Step 1: Gather Background Information

Brandon, an energetic 5-year-old boy, was adopted in Guatemala when he was a year old. His parents had been working there, had met him when he was in an orphanage, and adopted him, knowing that he was showing signs of having significant disabilities. He had several medical problems, including failure to thrive, which had since resolved. After spending several more months in Guatemala after the adoption was finalized, the family moved back to the United States, in part to provide quality medical care and education for him.

Brandon received early intervention services and began to make progress in many areas. However, his EI providers had suggested he might have autism in addition to his medical issues and developmental delays. At age 30 months he was diagnosed with autism and was enrolled in an intensive services program specifically for children with autism spectrum disorders. When he turned 3, those services ended, and he became eligible for services through the public school system.

Brandon did not thrive in the program. He became more withdrawn and quickly developed intense, self-injurious behaviors. Although his family could not be sure this was because of his placement, they had been hesitant about placing him in it in the first place, as it was not yet well established. They took him out of the program after observing the classroom several times and concluding that he was not getting the support and instruction he needed. They placed him in an integrated, university-affiliated, child-centered daycare program, which they felt was a more normalizing environment for him. The program also had the reputation for being culturally sensitive and family-oriented, which appealed to them.

Change in Program Leads to Initial Gains

Brandon did very well his first few years in the program. Both staff and family members noted that he was happy, enjoyed doing the pre-academic work and learned some daily living skills. He learned to follow directions and routines quickly, even though he did not develop any spoken language. Before his placement there, at around 3 years of age, he had developed an unusual fascination with automatic, pressure-sensitive electronic doors, such as one typically sees in supermarkets and department stores. He would pull away from his parents as they approached any store with this type of door and could get "stuck," sitting and blocking the entrances for long periods of time until he was lifted and removed, kicking and screaming, away from the building. Although this fascination continued, it was not as much of a problem at school, as there was only one such door—the elevator—which the staff could easily avoid when they were with him. Otherwise he exhibited few disruptive behaviors, and his self-injurious behaviors (head-banging, biting himself) largely disappeared.

As Brandon was the only child in the school with autism, his parents were able to obtain periodic consultation from an autism specialist through the university training program affiliated with the school. This specialist had set up a discrete trial/ABA program to teach Brandon academic skills. In his last year of preschool in the program, he had learned all the letters of the alphabet and acquired a large single-word receptive vocabulary through picture-matching programs. He appeared to enjoy these activities; he voluntarily sat at the table, waiting and smiling when staff members approached him, and he immediately engaged in work.

PECS Helps Nonverbal Student

Although he attended a private school, Brandon had access to a speech therapist through his public school system. She visited his program weekly, did some direct instruction with him, and provided feedback and suggestions to the staff. But Brandon remained nonverbal despite speech therapy and extensive exposure to language. He could make a few open vowel sounds but did not make consonant sounds. The speech therapist had suggested trying the use of pictures and the receptive picture identification program and to begin using the Picture Exchange Communication System (PECS), an augmentative/alternative communication system designed to teach individuals for whom spoken language is not adequate to initiate and sustain communication through the use of pictures.

Aside from his obsession with the doors, Brandon continued to be happy and compliant most of the time, both at school and at home. His parents and school staff thoroughly enjoyed him. He did not, however, engage in much social interaction with peers, but his classmates appeared to like him, and he seemed happy when he was around them. He was often seen playing near them, although not with them. Additionally, peers would help him by taking his hand if he did not naturally follow along with the group, and they would dance with him during group music and movement activities.

Step 2: Identify the Problem

Despite what family and school staff agreed had been excellent progress in preschool, a few months into his kindergarten year in the same program, Brandon began to develop new challenges. His school team was unable to solve them and asked for assistance. They wanted to support Brandon's development, especially in the area of speech, and they felt that his frustration with work was escalating. At the same time, his enjoyment in learning was diminishing, and his obsession with the electronic doors seemed to be increasing as well. His school and home team divided their concerns into four major categories:

1. *His refusal to follow directions, which seemed to come on suddenly.* Whereas he used to follow directions readily when he understood them, over that past month he had begun to appear to be deliberately noncompliant. For example, when staff asked him to "put your cup in the sink," he would take his cup and run the other way or put it in the toy cabinet and look back at the staff and smile. He did this both at home and at school.
2. *His diminishing enjoyment of academic activities.* Brandon had previously enjoyed matching and pointing to pictures, but he was no longer enjoying these tasks. Staff had begun teaching him to write letters, but he showed little interest. Worse, he became aggressive when told it was time to do his work, and he would sometimes rip up the worksheets or throw them on the floor.
3. *His fixation on the electronic doors continued and was becoming more of a problem outside of school, too.* He took frequent

walks in the community with his parents, and he knew exactly which buildings had electronic doors. So every family outing became a challenge; Brandon immediately bolted to the nearest door and would erupt in a major tantrum when his parents tried to get him to move on. As he was getting bigger and stronger and he lived in a busy urban neighborhood, keeping him and others around him safe was becoming more difficult.

4. *He was not making any progress in speech, and he had made only minimal progress in using pictures to communicate despite many hours of speech therapy.* Brandon continued to use nonverbal means, however. He had invented a few signs, which he used functionally. For example, he would tap on his wrist as if pointing to a watch when "arguing" about wanting more time for something.

Lagging Social Skills

The team did not identify social development as a problem, as Brandon and his peers liked being in each other's presence. However, upon further observation and questioning, Brandon had not really made gains in this area. His social interactions had not increased. He was not initiating with peers or adults, although his limit testing did reflect greater involvement with adults, including making more eye contact and smiling as he ran the opposite way.

Step 3: State the Working Hypothesis, Yours and Others'

Unfortunately, the autism specialist who had been available to the team earlier was no longer on staff. In fact, the university had closed its autism training program, and the school was in the process of searching for a new consultant. They decided to tackle the problems as a team, co-led by the speech therapist, who had the most experience with children with autism; the head teacher, who had the most experience with Brandon; and the parents, who were very involved in all aspects of Brandon's care and had a collaborative relationship with the school team.

They were all in agreement regarding what the problems were, although the intensity of each problem varied by setting. Doing work was more problematic at school, and the electronic doors were more problematic outside of school.

Regarding limit testing, both home and school describe this issue in the same way, with a very social component to it. Brandon's teacher believed this was the phase, similar to that of social 2-year-olds, of discovering the power of "limit testing." His gleeful social running was reminiscent of when she had worked in the toddler room in the program. Some of the children, when told it was time to go to their mats for a rest or time to go home, would dash in the other direction, exploding in laughter, making a game out of it. That Brandon had started to do this seemed to reflect an overall increased social connection and social desire, which was, in fact, a positive development. This also seemed to show he was understanding both what the adult wanted and that by doing the opposite he could predictably gain adult attention, reflecting increased social understanding. The family too reported he was trying to get chase and tickling games going with them more often at home.

Unintentional Positive Reinforcement

One staff person thought Brandon was becoming "manipulative." She expressed some frustration, assuming he was being defiant and disruptive on purpose. The head teacher explained that it probably was voluntary but not with the intent of annoying the adults or to be difficult, but rather, as a way to try to get attention and interact. Because he was largely nonverbal, it was one of the few ways he had found to achieve this goal, if in fact it was his goal.

The other staff helped by recalling that when he had started doing this, they had been so pleased to see him looking at them, making more eye contact, and smiling, that they had actually been reinforcing his behavior by turning it into a game of chase. So they were teaching him that if he continued this behavior, he could get a lot of attention and a good game of chase going!

After hearing about all of the problems and theories about them, the speech therapist asked more about the nature of the academic work. Last year, Brandon had been learning his letters, and one staff member suspected that he was actually able to read. Brandon's teacher wondered aloud if he was getting bored and was ready for more advanced academic work. So staff and family planned to further investigate his reading abilities, naturalistically, by showing him different words that he understood verbally, such as "snack" and "run," to see if he would respond appropriately to them. His teacher sometimes used a reading assessment with the other kindergarteners, including a subtest that measured one-word written vocabulary by matching pictures with words. She decided to use this format to evaluate Brandon's reading ability.

Regarding Brandon's objections to writing, his teacher and parents noted he was having great difficulty with more advanced fine-motor skills in several areas. These included buttoning and zipping clothing and assembling small Lego structures. He had not yet had an occupational therapy evaluation, and one could not be scheduled for another two months. However, it was clear he was having difficulty writing, and his team hypothesized that this very likely had a bearing on his reluctance and sometimes his absolute refusal to do work.

Academic Pressure, Even in Kindergarten

Staff also wondered if his increased frustration with work was in part because of the change in environment. He was required to spend a great deal more time on academic work in the kindergarten as opposed to preschool, where he spent far more time engaging in free play and physical activity. Perhaps he was required to sit, listen, and work for a stretch of time far exceeding his attention span. He was an active child who especially enjoyed running and climbing at recess.

Staff wanted to consider a major reduction in his work schedule, but the family was reluctant to give this up. They saw promise in his reading ability, which they felt was important to all areas of development but was especially critical for future communication options given his difficulties with spoken language. Hence, they could reach no consensus about how to intervene, although there was agreement on the necessity of further exploring possible causes of Brandon's problems.

Brandon's parents noted that his preoccupation with electronic doors had started shortly after they brought him home from Guatemala, at a time when he was beginning to crawl. He had a similar response to electric fans, and in the summer it was very difficult to avoid them. They were everywhere—at home, at friends' homes, in school, and in stores. Whenever he noticed one, he would stare at it happily, according to his mother, "as if in a trance." She continued, "I have a feeling that he would watch them all day if we let him." The team and family felt this was consistent with an obsession and decided to explore treatments for obsessions in children with autism.

Regarding Brandon's lack of speech development, everyone agreed he understood more and more words, despite his inability to speak. The speech therapist thought there might be a significant oral motor problem, such as apraxia, although she was not trained or experienced in working with children with this problem. The team continued to discuss all of the different hypotheses around each of the problem behaviors without dismissing any of them at this point.

Step 4: Review Treatment Approach(es)

At the end of the meeting, the team discussed some of the treatment approaches for each of the problems. For the limit testing, one component of the treatment included increasing time for social engagement with staff, including chase and other interactive, physical games. They would focus on more functional communication and teach Brandon to use a picture as well as a sign to initiate chase with adults, who would be certain to engage in chase with him whenever possible when he initiated.

The head teacher felt that providing other ways for him to gain an adult's attention and facilitating more social interactions with peers might diminish his attempts to gain social attention through limit testing. Furthermore, limiting the response around social bids for limit testing to minimal social engagement would likely make it less socially rewarding. So they also decided to facilitate chase games with peers at recess to ensure that he would have more positive social interaction, both to foster growth in this area as well as to diminish his limit testing.

Functional Communication Always Helpful

The speech therapist helped the team develop a "total communication" approach for teaching Brandon to request chase games, breaking down the task into very basic components. First he would need to get an adult or peer's attention by tapping them. Then they would teach him a sign (running arms) and show him a small photograph of himself laughing and running outside with peers. Staff shared these new systems with his peers so they could model and respond.

They also agreed to assess his academic levels in both reading/decoding and understanding written language. If it turned out he was reading words, they would immediately implement a plan for teaching more advanced reading tasks. Given the family's interest and the team's agreement that reading should become part of his communication system, staff decided to include primarily words that could be functional, including "no," "more," "chase," "door," "lunch," "I want," "No thank you," and so on. They would use the same words for reading work as in his Picture Communication and voice output systems and also decided to change the nature and quantity of his academic work: They would reduce handwriting demands and begin instruction in using the computer and keyboarding for composing simple assignments, believing that this may ease his frustration and improve his interest and ability to focus. If these changes were unsuccessful, they would consider a general reduction of work.

Adapted CBT (ERP) for Treating OCD

Regarding his obsession with doors, the head teacher did a search online for books about treating obsessive behaviors in children and came across Aureen Pinto Wagner's work, including *Worried No More* (2005), about using cognitive-behavioral therapy (CBT) with children. This sounded like it would require too much language to be effective for Brandon. She also reviewed several journals and found a few articles about exposure and response prevention (ERP), a component of cognitive-behavioral therapy that had been used with some success for typically developing children and children with autism.

She explained these principles to the team, and they recalled using a similar process a few years ago with another child who had been afraid of using the elevator, gradually enticing her to it while playing games and her favorite music. The team agreed this could be a promising approach and were willing to try it. Staff thought Brandon might be successful if, at the same time, they engaged him in highly desirable activities near the elevator, such as bubble and balloon play as well as chase. As detailed in Wagner's books and articles on ERP, they planned to begin at the opposite end of the hall farthest from the elevator and gradually work their way closer.

Brandon's parents didn't feel they would have success with this "exposure with response prevention" approach, as there were so many doors in their environment—at home, at school, and in the community—which he pulled toward whenever he spotted them. They didn't think they could set up and follow a consistent plan and also carry on with their regular routines and errands and get to the places they needed to go as a family.

Regarding Brandon's lack of progress with spoken language, the school team and family considered going to a hospital-based speech clinic specializing in working with children with autism, even though it was two hours away and the first appointment was not available for several months. In the meantime, the school speech therapist located a specialist in autism and apraxia, who worked in a program that also evaluated children for use of augmentative and alternative communication systems (AAC) that might include using pictures and electronic devices with voice output systems, as well as signing. The team had briefly talked about using this "Total Communication Approach" and decided that it could help Brandon develop more functional communication faster. They were reassured that his ability to use spoken language would not be impeded by using alternative methods, and in fact, it would likely be enhanced (Millar, Light, & Schlosser, 2006).

Brandon's parents explored this option and found that the expenses would be covered by their insurance plan. One of the therapists would be able to accompany the family to the appointment to help maximize home–school carryover, and the family was granted permission to videotape the session so they could further educate school staff. Additionally, Brandon's school speech therapist volunteered to videotape several sessions with Brandon so the hospital clinic could see what she was doing and how it was working in case Brandon did not "perform on command" during the evaluation.

Staff decided to take data regarding the frequency, intensity, and duration of his upsets around work, and of his location when he bolted toward the elevator. They made a five-point scale for recording intensity, by describing each point, culling from his repertoire of how upset he got, from not bothered at all to extremely upset. They used words and illustrations to represent each stage.

They would record frequency by simply counting the number of upsets, and duration by timing his upsets, and note the situation in which the tantrum occurred.

Some of the staff were concerned about introducing data collection, as they felt this would take away from time actually spent with Brandon and his classmates. As he was the only child in the class with autism, they were not as familiar with the concept of recording data. The speech therapist had taken data in her work with children with autism and developed simple and straightforward data sheets, which she duplicated and shared. In the beginning, formal data was collected only for those two areas.

Step 5: Design the Treatment Plan

Based on a review of the literature, staff experience and skill, and an exploration of what resources were available in the area, the team developed an initial treatment plan as they continued to assess the components contributing to the identified problems:

1. Use ERP strategies to decrease bolting to elevator behavior
2. Assess reading skills and level
3. Reinforce signing, PECS, or his voice output system
4. Decrease writing demands and add computer instruction
5. Record data regarding tantrum intensity, duration, frequency, situation, and on getting stuck at doors
6. Reconvene in three weeks to review the plan and determine amount of progress

Step 6: Evaluate Effectiveness and Generate Your Own Evidence

Limit testing in response to demands had decreased dramatically. The team evaluated the data and discovered that the staff had been inadvertently reinforcing Brandon's behavior by chasing after him every time he ran the other way. Once they began ignoring this behavior, it rapidly diminished.

At the same time, Brandon had been learning to use the picture for requesting chase, and the team had put several of these pictures in key places. They also placed one in Brandon's pocket that had a message recorded by a classmate. When pressed it said, "Play chase with me!", and he used it frequently. When he requested chase at inconvenient or inappropriate times, the staff had some difficulty helping him understand and accept this. However, he learned when and where his requests were reinforced, and he began initiating/requesting much more at recess and during breaks than during classroom instruction.

The team met three weeks later. Regarding Brandon's academics, the team discovered that in fact Brandon was reading, and not just a few words; he recognized and understood at least 40 sight words, which was close to his verbal receptive language vocabulary. The team agreed to institute a more advanced reading curriculum, and he began showing renewed interest in academic work. An added benefit was that Brandon's classmates began noticing him, commenting that "he's so smart," and tried to sit next to him and play with him far more often than before.

The team had also made a computer available to Brandon and began teaching him to use it in the classroom. He seemed to enjoy it, although he was not yet using it effectively for writing letters and words, but he was becoming familiar with the keyboard, experimenting with it and finding and playing various games. The team was not sure how to keep him from hitting the keys repeatedly, so it was not yet a productive means for structured academic learning. They decided to wait until after the clinical speech and language/AAC evaluation to determine if there were specific programs or approaches they could implement systematically, as they were now figuring things out as they went along and taking a more hit-or-miss approach.

Regarding exposure and response prevention work for elevator behaviors, Brandon had great fun playing games at a distance from the elevator, especially at the farthest end of the hall. But the very first time he spotted the elevator and heard the door opening and closing, he immediately bolted to it and disengaged from his teachers. After that, they were unable to play even remotely near the elevator, as he was so drawn to it. His parents noticed no difference in his preoccupation with elevators outside of school. They had not implemented any specific intervention and the school's treatment approach had not made a difference. So there was progress on all fronts except Brandon's obsession with elevators and electronic doors. However, a new problem had emerged as a result of his over-generalization of requesting chase.

The team looked at the data: Brandon's tantruming around work had diminished in frequency from two to three times during every work session to once following the changes made to his work structure. The team had not taken data on social interaction, as the autism specialist didn't want to overwhelm them with too much data collection. However, staff noted that Brandon was now enjoying playing chase with his classmates at recess, and that once he began initiating with them with staff facilitation, they began initiating with him as well. They started taking data periodically at recess regarding the frequency and length of his social interactions over the next few weeks.

Speech development was problematic. Brandon continued to have no vocalizations and used only the sign for chase, which he had learned very quickly and used spontaneously. So the team decided to introduce a few more pictures, using PECS and voice output push buttons (Bondy & Frost, 2001) for other high-motivation activities, and the family began using this approach at home as well.

The team reviewed the research literature on other approaches to exposure and response prevention and found one study on fear of physical exams in children with autism spectrum disorders (Gillis, Natof, Lokshin, & Romanczyk, 2009), in which exposure and response prevention was used with reinforced practice. They also found an article entitled "Stimulus Fading in Differential Reinforcement for the Treatment of Needle Phobia in a Youth with Autism" (Shabani & Fisher, 2006), in which a child was gradually exposed closer and closer to the needle while being given food. These studies were teaching children to not have a fear or avoidance response rather than to not have an approach response. They were not sure if this would work for Brandon's problem. Brandon's team decided that because he was highly motivated by food, they would try this as the "other" behavior to reinforce. They would use the "differential reinforcement of other" (DRO) paradigm, a technique for reducing problem behavior in which a reward is delivered contingent on the absence of the targeted behavior, in combination with exposure and response prevention for the automatic door obsession. They also continued with the other approaches they had put in place and monitored progress on all fronts.

OCD Proves Difficult to Treat

The team met two weeks later and reported several good outcomes. They had taken data on social interactions, and these were now happening for about half of his recess time. Brandon had learned when he could use a picture to request chase successfully and when it would not be successful, and he was requesting much less frequently during inappropriate times, such as during Circle Time or academic instruction. The enticement of food to keep him from bolting toward the elevator, however, had not been successful. His drive to approach the electronic doors appeared to be much stronger than his desire for food or for fun, motivating social activity. This continued to be a challenge at home as well, but the team had made headway in all of the other areas that were initially identified as problematic.

Step 7: Redesign the Plan as Needed

The team felt that although many of their interventions had been successful, a visit to Brandon's pediatrician for an evaluation and a discussion about possible medications to treat OCD would be useful. His pediatrician referred him on to a psychiatrist, and eventually his parents decided to enroll him in a research trial designed to assess the effectiveness of a specific medication in treating obsessive-compulsive disorder in children with autism. The team met a month after the onset of use of this medication and reported continued but substantially decreased intensity and frequency of his attempts to leave an activity or to bolt from his family toward automatic doors, and much less intense upsets when he was removed from the doors.

The team decided to reinstate their efforts with the exposure and response prevention, now that Brandon's drive had greatly diminished perhaps as a result, at least in part, of the medication. They then were so successful with this approach that they were soon able to take Brandon along with his class on trips around the school, during which they would pass the elevator several times without incident. At home the effects were not quite as robust, as there were so many different situations and routines, and no set schedule, so it was more difficult to be as consistent.

Overall, the treatment plan was considered a great success, and Brandon continued to thrive in this program for many months. The team eagerly awaited consultation with the hospital speech clinic for further input on Brandon's communication abilities, needs, emerging practices, and new communication devices, and with the occupational therapist for treating his fine-motor challenges.

CHAPTER 7

RAFAEL: A HAPPY, WELL-BEHAVED 6-YEAR-OLD BECOMES INCREASINGLY RIGID

"He seemed so smart when he was a toddler. Even though he got diagnosed with autism, I thought he'd do better and learn faster. I get discouraged sometimes. But yes, I do see some changes, some real progress. But it's never enough, is it?"

—Rafael's mother

Step 1: Gather Background Information

Rafael is a particularly attractive 6-year-old boy who lives with his parents, older brother, Pedro, and their two cats. He is frequently seen smiling, as long as he is doing what he likes to do: measuring things, such as the dimensions of the doors, windows, or tables in his kindergarten classroom, or drawing pictures of fans—ceiling fans, table fans, even industrial floor units.

Even before he was diagnosed with PDD-NOS at age 22 months, Rafael's parents knew he was different—delightful but different. At the time he wasn't talking at all and spent hours lining up objects, not only toy trains and cars, but also books, spoons and forks, and the mail. His parents remember how he used to dash to the front door every afternoon when he heard the mailman, practically snatch the envelopes right out of his hand, and line them up, from one end of the room to the other. "He seemed so happy and so purposeful," his mother recalls. We joked that he might end up working for the post office or for Federal Express. But, she continued, "We knew that other toddlers didn't do those things. They talked and played with regular toys and made car noises. And Pedro, who is only 2 years older, wasn't anything like Rafael."

Shortly after he was diagnosed, Rafael immediately began an intensive intervention program consisting of 20 hours per week of home-based, one-on-one ABA instruction, primarily discrete trials. This is what his early intervention program's specialty service provider recommended for all children under 3 who received an ASD diagnosis. Rafael made some major gains during the 14 months he spent in this program. He began to sign and then say some words; he was able to identify and match dozens of objects and pictures; and he began to count. He also recognized and could name the letters of the alphabet and even spelled his name with the magnetic letters on his refrigerator. His parents were encouraged; they began to realize that although he was different and seemed unaware of what was going on around him, he was smart. And most important, he was happy. But he didn't play with his brother. He barely noticed him.

Progress in Preschool

Rafael started attending a public, full-day, substantially separate program for children with a diagnosis of PDD/autism. He continued to receive ABA services at school, and he continued to acquire skills. He began to help dress himself. He learned to wash his hands and face and brush his teeth. He had a harder time with toilet training, which didn't really happen until the end of his second preschool year. He sat during Circle Time, lined up to go to the playground, and with varying degrees of assistance, was able to complete many classroom tasks and activities. Rafael's teacher constantly reassured his parents that "He is doing just fine. He's really no problem at all."

During Rafael's final year in preschool, still in a PDD classroom, some of his major strengths started to emerge. He showed considerable ability in drawing. He loved numbers and was especially attracted to rulers and tape measures, which he often carried around. And although he could say dozens of single words and sometimes used short phrases (e.g., "Want red crayon," "Daddy sit"), which his parents attributed to his ABA program, he only occasionally used them spontaneously. Most of the time, his teachers or parents would ask him yes-and-no questions, or ask "What's this?" or tell him to repeat what they said. Sometimes his language was meaningful; other times he was simply imitating.

By the time Rafael was about to transition to kindergarten, he was becoming far more rigid. He had always preferred certain activities, but in the past, his parents and teachers could get him to at least try others, such as playing percussion instruments, dancing, or tossing a ball back and forth. Not anymore. "Rafael became more and more obsessive about rulers and tape measures, and he only wanted to color or draw pictures. He rejected almost every other activity, at school and at home," according to his mother.

Rafael willingly participated in his daily DTT sessions and used the Picture Exchange Communication System (PECS) that was introduced at school and home to request and occasionally to comment, such as pointing to a picture of the sun and saying, usually with prompting, "It's hot." He continued to acquire self-care and daily living skills and was usually compliant. Each day he would hang up his backpack, get his lunch, feed himself, and put away his things when asked. With support, he would interact briefly with his classmates. But he only wanted to do the same few things: draw pictures, count and measure, or spell words. He was pleasant and well-behaved. His teacher continued to reassure his parents that he was well-liked and that he "fit in."

Rafael began kindergarten, which included a half-day in a small PDD classroom and a half-day in a larger, integrated program.

He continued on a similar trajectory—satisfied to do what he wanted to do and able to complete a few new tasks, such as doing puzzles and cutting out shapes. He continued with counting, naming letters, and drawing. However, his parents and now his school team were growing increasingly concerned about his limited interests and social indifference.

Step 2: Identify the Problem

Despite his many gains in preacademic learning and Activities of Daily Living (ADLs), Rafael was becoming increasingly rigid and obsessive. He played near but not with other children, and he only played with, or rather manipulated, the toys and objects he was interested in. He followed instructions, went to the dress-up corner, book corner, or playground, but unless a teacher was there to tell him, "Ask Josh if he wants to do a puzzle with you" or "Throw the ball to Erin," he would run off and count and measure things, with a real ruler if he had one, or if not, in a pretend fashion, using his hands. His classmates noticed how capable he was and actually encouraged him, often asking him, "How long is this?" or saying, "Guess how tall I am." However, they didn't seek him out to do the fun things, like playing house, superheroes, or Red Light, Green Light. He didn't tantrum and he wasn't aggressive. He simply had his own agenda. So really, one of the major problems was that he wasn't a problem!

Step 3: State the Hypothesis, Yours and Others'

On the surface, Rafael seemed to be doing well. He didn't have any aggressive or disruptive behaviors. He met most of the goals on his IEP. But he had no idea how to engage with his peers, unless the activity included measuring, numbers, or letters. And even then, he chose to do so alone. His ABA program got him jump-started, illuminated some of his strengths, and helped him learn many important skills, such as requesting, sequencing and completing activities, and following verbal directions and picture schedules. He seemed content.

Could it be that he didn't yet know how to share affect and attention? His parents and school team, especially his speech therapist, thought this was his major challenge and an ability he didn't have, one that he would not acquire through observation but would have to learn systematically.

Rule Out Depression

Or maybe Rafael was depressed. The district's autism specialist, a Board-Certified Behavior Analyst (BCBA) who had an elementary knowledge of mental health issues, thought that Rafael wasn't depressed, because he was often willing to do what he was told and didn't whine or cry. He spoke at length with the school psychologist, who did have training and experience in working with young children with depression and anxiety. She agreed that while Rafael's affect was flat much of the time in the classroom, he didn't display any of the typical signs of depression. Conversations with his parents and the rest of the staff indicated the same thing. He ate reasonably well; he slept well; he rarely cried; and he didn't look sad. He hadn't lost interest in formerly enjoyed activities.

The school psychologist considered the possibility that he had obsessive-compulsive disorder, which is often thought of as a symptom of autism, although it can also be a distinct, co-morbid condition. He reviewed the literature on autism, and on OCD and autism, and found that there was significant co-morbidity (e.g., Mattila et al., 2009). Although Rafael's behaviors appeared compulsive, one of the usual treatments for dealing with this anxiety disorder, such as cognitive-behavioral therapy (CBT), probably wouldn't be effective, as it would require far too much talk and reason.

Rafael simply couldn't access this approach at this time, because his speech was still so limited. Besides, the school psychologist felt that Rafael was "stuck" rather than obsessive-compulsive. She described the difference like this:

> The behavior looks the same, but the reason he plays with the same things in the same way are different. My gut feeling—and this is obviously not scientific—is that it is the result of being familiar and comfortable with certain activities and objects and having a mastery of them. He hasn't found any alternatives yet to measuring, counting, and spelling. He doesn't get any external or internal rewards for doing other things. He doesn't naturally observe his peers imitate or learn from them. To put it in very simple terms, Rafael's doing what he does best.

Many Theories, No Consensus

As is often the case, there was no consensus about why Rafael was behaving this way. But whatever the cause, Rafael's parents and teachers agreed he needed to expand his repertoire of activities, engage more with his peers, and stop measuring and counting so much.

Rafael's speech therapist had another theory. She pointed out that his language was increasing and improving, but he didn't know how to generalize, to become more spontaneous, ask questions, and make comments. He needed to learn how to have a conversation. She felt that he had all the basic skills but didn't know how to connect them. His OT, who had some training in Sensory Integration (SI), which is a term describing the brain's ability to organize and interpret sensory information, didn't feel that he was a "sensory kid." She elaborated on this, explaining that he didn't avoid, nor did he actively seek out, sensory stimuli to the extreme. He seemed to enjoy all of the activities during his OT sessions, such as jumping, swinging, playing at the water table, and in the bean box. She didn't think there was a major problem until other team members brought to her attention the fact that he was not really making progress in interacting with peers.

The team decided to consider all theories but to target Rafael's limited interests and lack of engagement with peers and then decide how to intervene. They also agreed that a lot was going right and that they didn't want to lose sight of the many gains he had made in a short time. They were also concerned that by putting additional pressure on him and pushing him to behave in ways that were unfamiliar, he might withdraw further.

Step 4: Review Treatment Approaches

The school's autism specialist met with Rafael's educational team, including his parents, and talked about the range of possibilities. There was no disagreement about his behaviors; everyone who knew or worked with Rafael was seeing the same things, both at school and at home. But they didn't exactly see eye to eye on several other issues. Rafael's parents wanted him to initiate more with them and his brother, to engage in "normal" play, to laugh with them, maybe even at them. His school team agreed that he wasn't yet very social, that his apparently obsessive behaviors were interfering with his making more social and even academic progress. They didn't know exactly how to address that problem in a systematic way or measure his progress.

The team also didn't agree about the underlying reasons or general approach to intervention. One of his teachers felt "that's just how kids with autism are. They only play with a few things." She pointed out that he seemed happy, and she thought he would maybe "outgrow" the problem. His special education teacher thought that putting a behavior plan in place might help: "If we give him more positive reinforcement for playing with other children or doing anything other than measuring, counting, and manipulating letters [what is called in behavioral terms Differential Reinforcement of Other (DRO)], maybe that will help broaden his interests."

The BCBA did a literature search on a variety of topics and cross-referenced them. He reviewed research on general approaches to treating autism, autism and repetitive behaviors, autism and OCD, and autism and depression. He also noted there were several recent books on treating OCD in children, although not in children with ASD (e.g., Wagner, 2002). He found a few studies on nonpharmaceutical treatments for OCD in children with autism (Wood et al., 2009), although most studies on this topic involved drug trials. He learned that, in general, different adaptations of CBT (and Exposure and Response Prevention or ERP) were used for typically developing children and some children with ASD, although there was not much information for children with ASD who were as young as Rafael. He felt he needed to test some of the approaches that seemed most related to what he and the rest of the team were observing.

Noncompliance Not an Issue

One of the complications was that Rafael's behavior (e.g., his interest in these topics) wasn't inappropriate—lots of parents of kindergartners would love for their kids to take a greater interest in numbers and letters—but the degree to which he engaged in them was. Furthermore, his obsessions were not directly interfering with Rafael's functioning in the sense that he complied, although somewhat reluctantly at times, with teachers' requests to do other things. However, his behavior did seem to be interfering with his own developmental progress, as he wasn't engaging in sufficient other activities or play to develop new skills. Rafael's behavior was also interfering with peer play, as he shared few activities or interests with his classmates. As they began to acquire new and more sophisticated play and academic skills, their interest in Rafael diminsished. So he was becoming more and more isolated.

The BCBA enlisted the support of everyone on the team and first conducted several school and home-based observations, although he didn't conduct a full functional behavioral assessment (FBA). Although an FBA may have been useful to identify if, for example, there were times when Rafael was more driven to these behaviors than other times and elucidating more information about possible functions, he felt that the time it would take to complete one would be better spent testing out some of the interventions. He decided this because Rafael's team and family agreed on what he did and at least accepted a general explanation of why he did this—because he enjoyed them—not as a reaction to some other aspect of his environment. Hence the BCBA didn't feel an FBA would yield helpful new information in this particular situation, and he went with more of a "try it and see" approach. He also reasoned that the interventions he would try were supported by a decent body of research, and that there was little potential for harm and a reasonable expectation that several interventions would be helpful.

The autism specialist did want to collect data and decided to record when and how often Rafael engaged in activities with numbers and letters, including measuring things, and quickly concluded that he did so when (a) they were available and (b) nobody "pushed" him to do something different. When there were other options, such as the availability of noisy toys, like a fire engine and an electronic wheel that made animal noises when the pictures were pressed, or an adult who was close by playing with other children and then pushed him to join in, he sometimes chose other activities.

At times he was reluctant, but with repeated efforts, he would participate without complaining or showing any signs of distress. At school, for example, when he started to measure things, he was usually redirected. The teacher or aide would present blocks, stack them, and tell him "Do this," which he often did, and which was then followed by verbal praise ("Wow! Good job! Cool tower!"). However, he didn't choose to play with the blocks at any other time. The BCBA pointed this out to the staff, that he actually wasn't as rigid as they thought, but he did need to be pushed, sometimes a great deal. His observations also confirmed that both staff and classmates assumed that Rafael would only want to measure or count, so they, consciously or not, made those activities more available to him.

The BCBA had some basic understanding of some of the play-based and relational approaches, although he had more training and experience with ABA. He suggested writing up some programs to increase Rafael's play repertoire, largely programs that would present several activities and then provide positive reinforcement for playing with toys and engaging in activities that were different from his usual play. Although Rafael's parents weren't opposed to reinforcing appropriate play and social behaviors, they wanted to try something different. They had also read about, heard about, and even watched a few videos on Floortime™ and high-affect play, and they also inquired about pivotal response training (PRT), which they felt would combine "the best of both worlds."

Parental Buy-In a Necessary Component

Their big concern was that they didn't want to "program" Rafael to behave in a specific way only because he would be rewarded, but rather, they wanted him to want to participate in other activities in other ways and truly enjoy it. They were also concerned that if he were taught specific ways to play with other materials he would object to the variations in play his peers might try to do with him. They were also worried that he might then extend his rigid activity to more materials without becoming more flexible in how he played. They had seen this at home when they had involved him in cooking to expand his interests; he wanted to cook the same way each time and became distressed with minor variations. The BCBA explained that even with the use of structured, behavioral interventions, Rafael would very likely learn to enjoy himself with other activities, over time, and not simply respond because he would earn a reward. He explained that the reward approach was an intermediate step to Rafael's developing enjoyment of new play skills and materials. Nevertheless, he felt that Rafael's parents had to buy into any plan if there was to be any expectation of success. If his parents were reluctant to carry out instructions, or worse, if they were skeptical, they might "forget" to follow the program; they might cut corners; or they might abandon the plan altogether. He reasoned that "if Rafael's parents are enthusiastic, they will spend much more time engaging in play with him, which is always good. They will probably introduce a variety of new activities, encourage him in subtle, perhaps immeasurable ways, and that in itself would be providing positive reinforcement."

Rafael's school team was very open-minded, and they looked forward to adding additional skills to their treatment options as well but pointed out how successful he had been with an ABA approach so far. They reasoned that ABA had a great deal of research support and was often presented as the first-line treatment for children with autism. They also felt that being able to measure progress in quantitative terms was a real plus.

Considering the parents' preferences, the BCBA reviewed some material from a workshop he had attended about using dramatic play as a way to teach and motivate teenagers with autism to interact socially. He found a few references, including the book *Acting Antics* (Schneider, 2007), which outlined many fun-sounding activities, although these were really meant for older children. He talked with the teacher about this and she brightened up immediately, saying that she used to use more drama games at morning meeting that she found in a book of activities for typical children, *On Stage: Theater*

Games and Activities for Kids (Bany-Winters, 1997), and other games she remembered from her own childhood and that the children in her neighborhood had loved playing.

The BCBA, upon hearing about these activities, noticed the similarities between these drama games, the *Acting Antics* activities, and some of the activities in a book about Relationship Development Intervention (RDI), an approach to teaching children to connect emotionally, created by Steven Gustein (Gutstein & Sheely, 2002). Although he hadn't gone through the RDI training process, he had read several articles and observed some certified RDI practitioners in action. He felt that this approach could also enhance Rafael's social/emotional development.

Step 5: Design the Treatment Plan

Rafael's entire team, including the BCBA, speech therapist, occupational therapist, special and general education teachers, school psychologist, and his parents, met. They looked over several studies on teaching play skills using all of the approaches they had reviewed and heard about. These approaches sounded like fun, and all members of the team had a positive reaction to what they read and learned. However, several members of the team had the impression that many of these approaches didn't have as strong a research base as ABA.

On the other hand, they agreed that adding another methodology didn't mean abandoning ABA. They weren't mutually exclusive. And, they recognized the importance of incorporating the family's preference. They had shared their major concerns about Rafael's overall flat affect and felt he might display more signs of happiness if more interactive and high-affect play were added to his routine. His parents also mentioned that they had been using the same sort of ABA approaches for a long time with Rafael, and while he had made many gains, he had not progressed in this particularly challenging area. They weren't ready to give up, and they weren't prepared to just wait and see.

So the team agreed to do the following:

1. Continue with some behavioral interventions, including monitoring Rafael's activities, especially during free play and other unstructured times, and presenting alternative toy/play options to his usual, limited repertoire of coloring, drawing, and measuring. Then they would reinforce his choices when he selected an alternative activity. They would record the number of times Rafael chose appropriate alternative activities, defined as manipulation of an available toy, other than crayons, markers, rulers, or tape measures, for more than 30 seconds, in relation to the number of opportunities. They would also keep separate records of the number of times he spontaneously chose appropriate alternative activities (i.e., without another person there, presenting toys or prompting).

2. Permit Rafael to play with his preferred objects (rulers, tape measures) on a limited basis, such as during part of the 15-minute "choice time" right after lunch, but only if he engages with one or several classmates at the same time. This would be facilitated by the classroom aide, who would also record whether he "stayed and played," chose another activity, or did "other," such as wandering off or refusing to play with anything or anybody.

3. When Rafael lined up toys and other objects, the team thought it would be enough to redirect him to another activity, and they would try to watch him more consistently. In the past they could usually get him to do something else, but they admitted that they didn't watch him every minute. When an adult wasn't present, he would drift back to his cars or blocks and continue lining them up.

4. In order to get Rafael to be more attentive to his classmates, more playful, and engaging in more physical and toy play with them, the team decided to use some fun social games that he and the other children would likely enjoy, which would foster shared positive interactions. They used some of the games from the teacher's book and some she played as a child. She also polled the staff, asking them to recall their favorite childhood games, and they would try some of those, too. In addition, she pulled and adapted some from the RDI book *Relationship Development Intervention with Young Children: Social and Emotional Development Activities for Asperger Syndrome, Autism, PDD, and NLD* (Gutstein & Sheely, 2002) and tried them out at his small group and during playground time.

5. Rafael would be assigned a "typical" student partner for some activities as well, although the partner might change every few days. For example, he and his partner would line up and go to the playground, get their snacks, and participate in their classroom jobs, such as being in charge of calendar activities, together. The thinking was that this arrangement would promote natural social interactions as well as imitation.

Rafael's speech therapist and special education teacher suggested that they should also look at and create a more sophisticated communication system, one that would be geared toward and draw on his cognitive abilities. Although his expressive and receptive language had been improving slowly, he didn't have a consistent and reliable method for expressing himself. They suggested making him a picture communication book that would allow him not only to request objects, toys, and food, but also to express spontaneous thoughts and opinions, and "talk" about people and events at home. A couple of the team members expressed their skepticism, however, arguing that

encouraging Rafael to use pictures instead of language would probably inhibit his speech. They worried that he would even "forget" the
words he knew. The speech therapist had often heard this argument
and was prepared with several research studies that demonstrated
the exact opposite, that using pictures or any other form of communication actually encourages spoken language (Tincani, 2004;
Sulzer-Azaroff, Hoffman, Horton, Bondy, & Frost, 2009). Her own
experience with dozens of nonverbal and minimally verbal students
over the past decade supported those studies.

So the staff put together pictures with labels and picture sentences, to enable Rafael to point to them and express himself, with
or without using spoken language as well. Pictures included the
people in his family, different types of weather, favorite and familiar
places, such as the local ice cream shop, corner convenience store,
gas station, movie theater, and playground, as well as common
objects and settings in his home and school (e.g., his bedroom, the
front door, the basement, and the flag pole in front of the school).
They didn't want to overwhelm him, just as he was getting more accustomed to using pictures to communicate. They sent the picture
communication book back and forth, from school to home, daily so
he could use the same system in both settings.

The team decided to convene again in a month and share their
initial experiences and impressions as well as present any quantitative data they had gathered.

Step 6: Evaluate Effectiveness and Generate Your Own Evidence

Although they originally had differences of opinion, everyone on
Rafael's team worked collaboratively. They followed their plan intensively for a month, checking in with each other and monitoring
some behaviors more closely and more formally than others. Their
first intervention, implementing a DRO program, appeared to work
well at school, but not as well at home. In more than 80% of

opportunities at school, Rafael chose alternative activities when they were presented, and he engaged with them for at least 30 seconds and up to 3 minutes. At home, however, his success rate was lower, choosing alternative activities only about 50% of the time when his parents made an effort to follow the protocol exactly. However, his mother and older brother Pedro reported that when they tickled him and teased him, like saying, "Oh, please, please, please, Rafael, please play ball with me," in a silly, whiny voice or even pretended that Rafael's Super Mario puppet was talking and pleading with him, he did respond and would join in playing ball or building with Duplo blocks for several minutes or more. They shot some iPhone camera videos and showed them to the team, who agreed that using behavioral methods along with silly, exaggerated affect in their play was a great combination.

Meaningful Play Leads to Social Gains

Rafael continued to choose rulers and tape measures during free choice time, but he was very open to having a classmate—or even many—join in. The classroom aide facilitated their interactions. She helped Rafael go around the class and find out how tall several peers were by having them lie down on the floor and then measuring them. This led to a lot of laughter, with one boy pretending to go to sleep and another pretending to swim away. The aide helped another child write down the children's heights on the blackboard, which led to a variety of fun learning activities, such as practicing writing numbers, comparing heights, and having students line up in ascending and descending order. The team decided to continue on this trajectory when Rafael chose his favorite activities, but they did not permit him to measure and count alone. They also continued to present other options, which he occasionally chose during free choice time and they reinforced those choices with social praise, which he began to enjoy and even seek out.

Reducing Rafael's lining up objects was a more difficult challenge. When he wasn't actively engaged, he did seem to default to lining up cars, trucks, trains, blocks, balls—anything and everything. The trick was to keep him engaged in other productive toy and interactive play. This was often possible at school but not as easy at home, because his parents couldn't play with him during every waking moment, and his brother was beginning to have real homework. However, another intervention that had worked well was the communication book that Rafael's speech therapist had been putting together, with help and suggestions from the entire team. He was getting far more competent in using pictures to communicate, primarily by requesting, but increasingly making comments and answering questions.

Picture Schedules Help

With team support, Rafael's parents built on his previous success with picture communication and decided to create a visual schedule of activities for him to follow when he got home. It was similar to the visual schedule posted at school, which was duplicated in his communication book. Using it, he could work on and improve many skills, including following directions, sequencing activities, and sampling new and less preferred activities. With a lot of training and providing a great deal of positive reinforcement, both in the form of social praise and some favorite treats, such as gummi bears, Rafael's obsession with lining up objects began to diminish slowly. His parents hadn't taken any formal data yet, but they were encouraged by their own observations and invited the BCBA to observe and perhaps set up a more formal structure and keep records of how and when he used his picture schedule.

Rafael also responded well to having a peer partner, although he didn't imitate him as much as the team had hoped. The teacher experimented with several peer partners and found that one, in particular, a rather loud, slightly hyperactive boy, brought out the best in Rafael. Although he wasn't imitating the boy, Rafael was becoming far more attentive. He watched him constantly, even when they weren't partnered for a particular activity and even if he was on the other side of the room. Rafael's parents noticed that he was becoming more aware of his brother at home, too. He looked for him when he got home from school and smiled at him at the dinner table, but he still didn't initiate or really play with him. That was the next big goal—and big challenge—that his parents wanted to tackle.

The communication book had many advantages: (1) Rafael would look through it and sometimes point to pictures and whisper to himself, even when he wasn't actively engaged in communication with an adult or peer; (2) he did increase his spoken vocabulary slowly, acquiring 15 more single words in the first 6 weeks; and (3) he became gradually more able to use increasingly complex expressions, by pointing to pictures of a car, his mother, and the front of the school. When this happened, his peers would try to interpret what he was saying, for example, "Is your mother picking you up in the car? Or are you saying she dropped you off at school?" Many of Rafael's classmates expressed a tremendous joy when they "got it," which they knew by his positive facial expressions and vocalizations. They also enjoyed using his book themselves and pointed to pictures to talk to him and to each other. This delighted the teacher, as she could see her classroom becoming a real community.

The drama games were also deemed a success with Rafael, his classmates, and his teachers. The staff noticed how Rafael perked up and stayed focused during these games, and they felt the games were helping all of the children to be more in tune with each other. His teacher noticed some carryover to recess a few times with a small group of children who worked hard to get Rafael to join them in playing a couple of the games, using the same scripts and actions.

Although some of the interventions were working some of the time, in some settings, and very slowly much of the time, creating a functional communication system proved to be far more successful than anyone had anticipated. The team decided to build on their success with the communication book, to play to his strengths, and to think about ways they could harness and use them to address some of Rafael's other behaviors. They noted a pattern in their treatment plan successes: The team agreed that his very positive response to the dramatic games and to his family's high-affect play at home shared the quality of positive, playful, emotional connections within a structure that was easy for Rafael to understand and enjoy. They agreed to continue the approaches that were having a positive impact, and the BCBA decided to get advice from a colleague who was starting a drama program in another state for children with ASD, so he too could take advantage of this approach and try out some of his latest ideas.

Step 7: Redesign the Plan as Needed

Rafael's team planned to continue to monitor his progress using all of the interventions that were successful. They continued to use ABA-based methodology but infused into it more reciprocal games, dramatic play, and cooperative activities. They also planned to slowly introduce increasingly more complex language and concepts into his academic work. In addition to supporting his social/emotional development, they planned to increase the focus on his academic preparedness for first grade.

CHAPTER 8

ALEX: EXTREME MOOD DYSREGULATION INTERFERES WITH SCHOOL AND HOME FUNCTIONING FOR A FOURTH GRADER

"We know *he can do the work, he's a really smart kid, so why does he totally fall apart when we give him work to do?"*

—Alex's teacher

Step 1: Gather Background Information

Alex is a handsome, talkative 10-year-old who lives with his parents and Golden Retriever. He was diagnosed with Asperger's syndrome before age 3 and is now a fourth grader attending a regular inclusion classroom. He is one of 20 students in the class and the only student with an ASD diagnosis, although there are three other students with learning disabilities. The school has had quite a bit of experience with Asperger's, as they had several other students in other grades with autism spectrum disorders, and they have an Asperger/autism support program within the district. Most of the children have more severe autism symptoms than Alex, but Alex has been having significant behavioral challenges, which have recently escalated.

Alex's educational team asked Ms. Garrison, the school psychologist, to get more involved and consult on his case, as his symptoms were so severe and bizarre, there was concern that Alex might be having psychotic episodes. She met with Alex in her office, initially with his parents. He was very quiet and withdrawn, and he made little eye contact. His parents said he had not slept well the night before, and he had been extremely anxious about the appointment. It was difficult to discern what he was like, apart from his being in obvious emotional distress throughout the visit. However, she was able to get his parents' perspective, and their concerns were similar to the school team's. They too wondered if he might be having intrusive thoughts, as he sometimes made very odd, frightening, and out-of-context statements. They also reported, as the school had, that he had become increasingly aggressive, whereas he had not been in the past. He was rarely aggressive at home but things began to change about three months ago. They noted that he had a few friends in the neighborhood, whom he had known since the family moved to the area when he was in preschool, and he occasionally got together with them. But he no longer got together with classmates from school as he had as recently as last school year.

Observation Sheds Light on Strengths and Challenges

Ms. Garrison observed Alex at school for two hours and then met with his team. The school and family agreed that his strengths included art projects, especially drawing, music, and dance. He had a strong dislike of tests, especially those involving writing. He seemed very distracted during classroom instruction, and it was during those occasions when the decontextualized statements were heard most often, particularly during full class lectures and review sessions. For example, when his teacher started to explain a math unit on long division, Alex announced that he was going camping with his cousins next month and described in great detail, almost lectured about a similar trip he took with them several years ago when a huge rain storm blew down their tent. His classmates were puzzled and his teacher was slightly alarmed. Alex was completely oblivious to their reactions and continued with his story.

Alex was not able to participate in any group work. He got angry and aggressive when any demands were placed on him, including simple tasks that he previously would have at least attempted. His teachers were growing frustrated and impatient with him, although they agreed that they knew his behaviors weren't intentional. However, they were at a loss, as they knew that he could do the academic work. Yet when it was placed in front of him or when he was asked direct questions about his reading or to show his work on a math problem, he would either run out of the room or yell in protest. If staff went after him and tried to redirect him back to class, he flailed his arms and tried to hit them.

At recess Alex's classmates began to avoid him. Staff speculated that they were scared of his unpredictability and aggression. He was increasingly playing by himself and only rarely with other children, usually younger ones.

Step 2: Identify the Problem

This was a complicated and disturbing situation, according to staff, with several different types of problems to solve. First, there was some concern about a possible thought disorder, taking into consideration his bizarre ruminations and decontextualized statements made at home and school, during all class periods. Then there was the issue of aggression and noncompliance, especially in response to work tasks. He was experiencing increasing social isolation, primarily at school. Fortunately, Alex continued to play with friends in the neighborhood after school and did not get angry or aggressive with them. But he refused to do academic work. When his parents offered to help him, he exploded, screaming, swearing, and sometimes throwing his backpack and books on the floor.

Step 3: State the Hypothesis, Yours and Others'

There was a great range of hypotheses among different members of Alex's team and his outside providers. The team had conducted a Functional Behavioral Assessment (FBA) and found that his non-compliance and aggressive behaviors were escape-motivated around academic work, yet this seemed to be confusing and contradictory. In the past he liked academic work and sought out challenges. It was relatively easy for him, and formal testing had indicated that he was a bright child, above average in every academic area.

The school team felt that not enough limits or demands were being placed on him at home, so his behavior was better there. He was free to do as he pleased. That also explained why he was having so much trouble with limits and demands at school, they thought. On the other hand, the family felt that the school did not give him enough choices or understand him, and that was why he was having so many behavior problems at school. However, the family felt that his behaviors were beginning to escalate at home, too. There was some degree of anger, frustration, and blaming across the family and school team, but all were highly motivated to try to work together. First and foremost, all were very concerned about and committed to Alex.

Ms. Garrison had several hypotheses. She wondered if Alex was depressed and acting out as a manifestation of depression, perhaps secondary to social isolation that was occurring at school but not at home. She also wondered if he might actually be displaying the beginning symptoms of psychosis, as there is sometimes misdiagnosis or an evolution of a diagnosis from an Asperger's disorder diagnosis. She consulted the research literature, and while onset of psychosis may be reported before age 11, this is quite rare (e.g., Eggers, Bunk & Krause, 2000). However, it was not unheard of, and she felt it would be important to rule out a thought disorder.

No Positive Peer Interactions

Staff observations were consistent. Alex's teachers and the psychologist formed similar impressions, that Alex had almost no interactions with peers outside of his weekly half-hour social skills group and that there were recurring instances of inappropriate social attempts on Alex's part. These included behaviors such as yelling out random, irrelevant comments in class and sticking his finger in his nose and looking around at his peers while laughing loudly. Once he pulled up his shirt in the classroom, looked at his classmates for a reaction, and burst into hysterics. Ms. Garrison hypothesized that Alex was very much trying to connect with his peers and did not know appropriate ways to do this. His behaviors were definitely getting their attention, and he was getting dramatic responses, albeit negative ones, so he did them repeatedly.

Ms. Garrison also wondered if there were aspects of his assignments that were too difficult. Maybe the increasing length, complexity, and organizational requirements of his English language arts class were overwhelming or confusing to him. Or possibly refusing to do work was one of the few aspects of Alex's day that he was able to control and more a manifestation of an overall level of frustration than a reaction to increasing academic demands.

Ms. Garrison wondered about his use of decontextualized statements during group instruction and if he was possibly having difficulties with processing the language at the pace or abstraction level of fourth grade. She knew from her experience that this was not uncommon for students with the learning disability profile often seen in children with Asperger's disorder and can easily result in inappropriate responses and irrelevant comments.

Seeking Out Opinions Yields Additional Information

In the process of formulating hypotheses, Ms. Garrison realized she had forgotten to question the team in more depth. She went back and asked if there were times during the day or specific circumstances during which Alex was most likely to be socially appropriate and successful, knowing this might shed further light on what was driving his behaviors. The team leader indicated that he was most successful (i.e., appropriate, relaxed, willing to participate) during his social skills group. They were using the Social Thinking curriculum developed by Michelle Garcia Winner (2008), led by the speech therapist, and he was truly enjoying this group, which met twice weekly. He rarely had behavior problems and participated regularly. He initiated more often with peers, asked and answered questions, and sustained longer interactions. Within this context the speech therapist had been able to identify some situations in which Alex could relate to some of the characters from Garcia Winner's "Superflex" curriculum. He was also more engaged and interactive within these groups. Five other students attended and Alex got along with all of them.

The speech therapist posed the same question to Alex's family, although they had previously identified several other situations in which he was successful. He began taking a music class in the Fall but was starting to have similar behavior problems there and had to drop it. For example, he yelled out when other students were playing instruments or singing, and he wouldn't follow group instructions. The family thought he was being actively defiant. Last year he had taken karate and was reasonably successful, but he complained that it was boring, didn't want to continue, and his parents didn't push him, so his extracurricular activities had come to a screeching halt. Alex's "best times" were when he was alone, drawing, dancing to the songs in his extensive iPod library, or playing computer games. His parents indicated that he also enjoyed playing with one or two children in the neighborhood, although he was beginning to have some major disagreements with them, too, and seemed to be gravitating toward their younger siblings.

Still puzzled, Ms. Garrison asked more specifically about the nature of his inappropriate statements in class. Alex's special education team leader noted that she had been most concerned during episodes of aggression, which always occurred when academic demands were placed on him. His teacher would take him to an empty therapy room to calm down after he yelled out that he hated work, hated school, or made similar loud and negative statements, disrupting the entire class. Once he lay down on the floor and said he was invisible and nobody would ever see him again. This really worried the staff and especially his team leader, who had already been concerned about major depression, but she had also considered a thought disorder.

Alex made other irrelevant statements, but these were less concerning, since they were scripted from a current popular movie that he had watched many times. He would occasionally repeat a punchline from the movie in a silly voice, then laugh and look around. Staff wondered if he was thinking he was in the movie during those times, or if this was just a way to get social attention.

Ms. Garrison had another meeting with Alex and his family to more directly address the issue of psychosis. She hadn't seen or heard anything besides the unusual statements, which usually surfaced when he was stressed or not attending during large-group instruction. But she wanted to more carefully assess his symptoms, due to its seriousness and the need for immediate intervention.

Ms. Garrison used the K-SADs (Schedule for Affective Disorders and Schizophrenia for School-Age Children; Birmaher, Ehmann, Axelson, et al, 2009) assessment tool and a clinical interview base to explore a possible thought disorder. She asked Alex if he ever heard people talking when there was no one there, and he said, "In my head I think about Angry Birds (a popular iPad app/game that he enjoyed playing), and I think of the sounds of the birds, and it's so cool when they smash into the pigs!" Then he added, "Sometimes when I'm going to sleep I hear the TV on downstairs but nobody is in my room." His relatively concrete understanding of the question and his difficulty staying on topic made the interview less than valid. However, on questioning him and his parents further, there were no other suggestions of a thought disorder or schizophrenia diagnosis.

Mood Issues Considered

Ms. Garrison continued to be concerned about depression, although Alex's parents reported that he was generally cheerful at home, especially when he played computer or video games or outside with friends in the neighborhood. But when it came to doing homework, he immediately became angry and upset. This indicated that he might be discouraged about his lack of success at school but was not clinically depressed overall.

Alex's parents continued to track and ponder his behaviors. It occurred to them that they had never talked with him about his diagnosis of Asperger syndrome or about his differences. His school team also said that they had not approached the subject either, nor had they ever had general discussions with the class about autism, Asperger's, or any other disability. The only formal instruction Alex and his class had was one all-school assembly on learning differences, which was held each Fall shortly after school began. Neither Alex nor his classmates had related this information to Alex himself.

Was refusing to do work a way to gain some control over his school days, where he was spending most of his time and experiencing so much social and academic failure? Or was there something about the his assignments that was really too hard for him? Or could it be some combination of factors?

Step 4: Review Treatment Approaches

Ms. Garrison was familiar with the scant literature on treating depression in individuals with Asperger's, and the literature on the incidence of depression and its correlation with social isolation in individuals with the diagnosis. She felt, as did his school team and parents, that increasing Alex's social connections and social success was a high priority in developing a treatment plan.

The literature on the efficacy of social skills groups was also limited. However, the fact that he was doing so well in this group was important when considering in what kinds of situations he was happiest and relaxed, behaved well, and talked in a more typical fashion. Perhaps adding more social skills groups to his program or even reconstructing his whole program to look and feel more like the social skills group would help.

Ms. Garrison was also familiar with the high incidence of difficulty with both processing speed and processing abstract material identified in children with Asperger's. She considered trying to eliminate large and long group lectures from Alex's day and instead place him in smaller groups that were taught the same material. She and the team needed more detailed information about his language processing and cognitive processing of abstract information in order to determine if there were aspects of the curriculum/class material or presentation style that he wasn't able to follow.

Initiating Discussions About Asperger's

Ms. Garrison recommended initiating discussions about Asperger's with Alex as well as with his peers so everyone had a better understanding of Alex—his differences and especially his considerable strengths and particular challenges. She had had many positive experiences with open discussions of students' disabilities, which helped them and others to better understand, accept, and even embrace some of their social differences, and she felt this would be a positive step.

Alex's parents had some reservations about talking to him about Asperger's. They worried that labeling him would further upset him and lower his already fragile self-esteem. But Ms. Garrison pointed out that he was already aware of his social frustrations and failures, and that helping him understand his strengths and challenges and knowing there were many other children with this diagnosis might actually improve his self-esteem. Perhaps meeting other children and adults through an Asperger's organization would also help him feel better about himself, lead to new friendships, and might allow him to accept his differences and reframe them as being unique characteristics, rather than internalizing the differences in a negative way.

She directed the school and family to a few books dealing directly with children's understanding of Asperger's (Attwood, 2006; Bromfield, 2011) and to some YouTube videos of children and teens with Asperger's talking about their diagnosis. She brought in some books written especially for children for Alex's parents and teachers to look over, including *This Is Asperger Syndrome* (Gagnon & Smith Myles, 1999), *What It Is To Be Me!: An Asperger Kid Book* (Wine, 2005), and *Different Like Me: My Book of Autism Heroes* (Elder & Thomas, 2005).

Ms. Garrison also suggested that Alex's parents contact or at least learn about the regional Asperger's Association and that at some point Alex could benefit from joining a formal group with other children with Asperger's. She was aware that such groups met regularly, participated in community activities, and went on field trips.

Alex's parents and some of the other team members were concerned that this information might make him feel "even more different," but Ms. Garrison related her previous experiences with children, explaining that every one of them ended up feeling much better, even relieved, once they got a better understanding of Asperger's and met others with the same challenges. She informed the team that many adults with Asperger's use the term "Aspie" to proudly describe themselves and how many successful adults, such as the author and speaker Lianne Holiday Willey, found it helpful to have connections with other people with Asperger's and wanted to spare others the isolation they experienced as children. Willey talked about how there were some similarities to the deaf culture/deaf community pride movement and many other populations who feel marginalized or just plain different.

Alex's parents were still somewhat reluctant, but through ongoing discussions and reading several books and articles dealing with this subject, they began to see the potential benefits for Alex and the entire family in opening up discussions.

Step 5: Design the Treatment Plan

Unfortunately, at this point, Ms. Garrison's consultation was considered complete by the team, as she had been contacted specifically to rule out psychosis, and funding for additional consultation wasn't available. However, the school did have funding for a part-time autism specialist, and the team worked together to identify a social worker whose specialty was treating school-aged children with Asperger's and convinced the school to hire him.

The team then designed a treatment plan that included:

1. *Arranging for Alex to have weekly meetings with the social worker,* who could further explore self-esteem and self-perceptions with him, as well as work with his family in helping him become aware of his diagnosis—if that's what they all decided to do. The new social worker also agreed to meet regularly with team members and give them tips and suggestions for supporting Alex throughout the school day.
2. *Fostering more social peer connections and friendships.* The team suggested adding two more social skills group sessions, so Alex could join in with peers he knew from lunch and recess, as this structured format had been so successful for him.
3. *Organizing academic instruction in a smaller group format, similar to what was already in place for children with learning*

disabilities. They speculated that this would decrease his frustration around work as well as increase his social contacts.

4. *Increasing afterschool playdates with a few children with whom Alex had had relationships in the past,* as he was more successful socially at home than at school.

5. *Recording data both at home and at school, on the frequency, intensity, and duration of Alex's upsets, as well as recording the number and duration of his peer interactions.* This would involve a cooperative effort between Alex's parents and school team, but both agreed that it would be worthwhile.

6. *Adding another social skills group outside of school, specifically for children with Asperger's disorder.* Alex's parents and team agreed that if he could find some children who shared some of his experiences and frustrations, this would help him feel less isolated and increase his sense of belonging.

Up-to-Date Evaluations Inform Decision Making

To get a better understanding of Alex's academic performance, the team recommended an updated speech and language evaluation to explore the issue of Alex's inattention to large-group instruction, with a particular focus on his rate and level of language processing. They also recommended a neuropsychological evaluation, but the school did not have a neuropsychologist on staff, and this kind of testing was not covered by the family's insurance. Ms. Garrison offered to do a psychological evaluation, which would get at some of the issues related to Alex's learning style, although not in as much detail as a full neuropsychological evaluation. All felt that a general psychological assessment, in combination with a thorough speech evaluation, would add some insight into Alex's learning style and strengths.

The autism specialist developed a simple data collection sheet for the team to use in tracking the frequency, intensity, and duration of Alex's objections to work and aggressions and also his tangential statements.

Step 6: Evaluate Effectiveness and Generate Your Own Evidence

After several weeks in the smaller classroom, Alex's behavioral outbursts significantly decreased. He continued to object and complain when he was assigned work, although far less frequently, and he no longer had huge emotional outbursts. His aggressions ceased completely. Peer interactions outside of the social skills group at school did not increase. At home he continued to play with neighborhood children.

Alex quickly formed a strong alliance with his school social worker. However, he continued to have limited insight into his school experiences and relationships, except to comment, "Nobody likes me and I don't have any friends." He was generally cheerful during his therapy sessions and did not seem to be depressed except when talking about school, which he was reluctant to do. During those conversations, he averted his eyes and teared up.

The team reconvened a month later to review the results of the testing and discuss the impressions and recommendations provided by Alex's social worker. The results of the speech evaluation indicated that while Alex's vocabulary and sentence length were above average for his age, his rate of language processing was two years below grade level. His comprehension of material involving abstract content also lagged two years below grade level. This applied to both his reading comprehension and oral language processing. These deficits were impacting his ability to attend and participate in whole-group instruction, and at least partially explained his use of decontextualized statements in such circumstances. His language processing profile also may have explained his increased objection to completing academic work, although it was still unclear as to why his reactions were so dramatic.

Several likely explanations for his extreme behavior remained. For example, he might have been frustrated with schoolwork in general, as he was having so little success, or as the psychologist had initially hypothesized, this might have been a very concrete way of exerting control or expressing his confusion or annoyance because he couldn't understand what was being taught in the classroom.

A Closer Look at Friendship

Alex's social worker relayed his frequent comments about not having any friends and his sadness whenever the subject came up, which did not surprise the team. They also felt he was becoming increasingly lonely and isolated and were more convinced than ever that his negative social behaviors were misguided attempts to connect socially with his peers.

It was still unclear why Alex was not making more friends within the small class, as it was much easier for him to function there and he seemed more relaxed than in the larger, general education class. The teacher of the small class indicated that most of the other children had learning disabilities, many in the milder range, but were more or less typical in other ways. They were socially sophisticated, found it easy to joke around with each other, and had an interest in sports, movies, and other age-appropriate activities. When Alex tried to make a joke or comment about what he had done over the weekend, he often just "missed the mark," and the rest of the group was at a loss as to how to respond. For example, at lunch one day, as his peers were joking around about their baseball's team's recent loss with the embarrassing score of 15–1, Alex chimed in loudly, "Speaking of losing or rather NOT losing, to be more precise, I finally beat that whole Angry Birds game. Can you believe it?" Although his peers didn't exactly tease him, their responses were brief and dismissive, and they carried on with their conversation about baseball. He probably sensed this, and he continued to have difficulty joining in conversations and making connections with typical peers, even within this smaller setting.

Alex's mother pointed out that he consistently had positive social interactions at home with friends from the neighborhood. She also noticed that the two children he played with most often, two sisters who lived next door, were children he had known since he was a toddler. So they had a common history and a vast repertoire of activities and games, which the three of them had invented and enjoyed for many years. They chased each other around their pool, played hide-and-seek, and caught fireflies together on hot summer nights. Alex found it much easier to participate in these activities than the more language-based and complicated social interactions and fast-paced conversations that typically occurred at school.

Alex's parents reported he was doing well in his Asperger's social skills group. He had even made a few real friends there. And, he had not had any behavior problems! His parents noted that he appeared more relaxed, spontaneous—much more typical when interacting with the children in this group. They felt this was because several of the children shared his interests and quirky sense of humor. As all of the children were "different," Alex didn't stand out, which they felt he himself perceived. In fact he mentioned to them that "this is the most normal group of kids I've ever been with." It wasn't clear if the small group size and nature of activities were helping him succeed or if it was the fact that he had more in common with these children. Whichever the case, Alex looked forward to returning to the group each week, told his parents detailed stories about what they did, and talked about and laughed about the group, which thrilled them.

As a result of this successful experience, Alex's parents and school team became more comfortable about bringing up the subject of Asperger's, and his social worker agreed that he was ready. They all thought it would be helpful to also initiate discussions with his peers. As it turned out, the program director at Alex's outside social skills group had been diagnosed with Asperger's as a child, and he offered to talk with Alex about it. His group was a natural place to begin, as many of the children openly talked about having Asperger's. In fact, Alex came home one day and asked his parents what it was. Furthermore, the program director offered to come in to the school and talk to Alex's class, along with Alex, about Asperger's, using funny videos and stories from his own life and making it an upbeat, positive introduction to the topic.

Alex's negative behaviors had greatly diminished at school over the past month. The team agreed to continue the plan and meet again in a month. At the next month's meeting, actual collected data and casual observations indicated that Alex's negative behaviors had begun to increase again, to the point of aggression. These incidents occurred largely in response to academic demands, even though he had some initial success within the small group. But social relationships had not improved significantly at school, and negative social behaviors were reappearing.

The school social worker continued to report that Alex was cheerful during their sessions, that he talked happily about a variety of experiences and activities outside of school, and he sometimes talked about his schoolwork. But he continued to express sadness and disappointment when he talked about how other children at school did not like him and that he was "the least popular kid in the entire school." He said that one child had called him weird.

Asperger Pride

Alex had become increasingly comfortable with the term Asperger's, and he even wanted to make a video about it for the local access TV station "to educate the public because people just don't get it." His family heard from one of the parents in his social skills group about a private school with all small classes, in which many of the students had Asperger's. This parent reassured them that the children were bright, got very good academic instruction, and participated in lots of social groups, including problem-solving sessions. Some of the students spent a year or two at the school and then returned to their public schools, and some went on to small private high schools. Alex's parents had never considered a private school but decided to visit. They were impressed with the training and experience of the staff and especially their commitment to children "just like Alex."

Again, while the school team felt he was making some progress, his increase in behavioral challenges was concerning to them, and they agreed to explore the private school option. They worried that Alex would lose out on the experience of inclusion and the district's many academic and recreational opportunities, but they admitted that he might be more comfortable, open to learning, and experience more social success at a private school.

In the meantime, Alex's parents enrolled him in a science game club outside of school that they heard "through the grapevine" catered to children with Asperger's. He also continued with his social skills group. Alex's parents wanted to see how he would do in another Asperger's-oriented environment, as sort of a test case before actively pursuing a private school placement. They were very torn, as they had always hoped that Alex would be able to thrive in and graduate from their local public school.

Step 7: Redesign the Plan as Needed

At this point, Alex's academic challenges had been clarified, and they were being addressed. Some, but not all, of his behavioral challenges had decreased, but his social isolation was now the primary issue. The school and family would need to discuss his placement. Could his social/emotional needs be met in his current setting? Would a specialized private school program be beneficial for Alex, and would it provide "a free and appropriate education in the least restrictive environment," which is mandated by federal law? This became the major issue for the next phase of the plan.

CHAPTER 9

EMILY: A PASSIVE TEENAGER BEGINS TO LEARN SELF-HELP SKILLS

"I don't care if she is autistic . . . or whatever. She can't hog the TV all the time, and she should still pick up her stuff in the bathroom, just like I do."

—Emily's sister, age 10

Step 1: Gather Background Information

Emily, a 15-year-old girl with a diagnosis of autistic disorder, lives with her parents and 10-year-old sister in a large, working-class suburban town. She displayed global delays during her first 18 months of life and was diagnosed with autistic disorder at age 2. Between ages 2 and 3 she received intensive early intervention services, including speech and language therapy and occupational therapy, and she also attended an early intervention playgroup. During that year, however, she made very little progress across all domains. Her parents grew increasingly concerned at that time and enlisted the help of several providers. They put into place a 25-hour-a-week ABA program that included some work at the early intervention center, with the majority of hours spent in one-on-one home-based sessions.

Emily began to make some progress in this ABA program, but at a very slow rate and only in some areas. For example, her diet had been extremely limited, and she began trying and enjoying a few new foods. She went from drinking out of a bottle to using a sippy cup. Before beginning this program, she had no interest in other people or toy play, but within a few weeks she began to look when her name was called, and she showed some interest in new and novel toys. However, she did not play with them in the typical fashion, and her interactions with others, both adults and children, continued to be very limited. She smiled and reached for her parents and her sister, but she didn't seem to notice or respond to other people.

At age 3 Emily transitioned to a small, substantially separate preschool program in the local school district. There were five other students in her class, all with autism spectrum disorders. She attended that program for more than two years, continuing to make slow, steady progress. She began to use basic picture communication (PECS) to indicate things that she wanted, such as blocks, chips, or juice, and she was able to recognize and point to pictures of her family members, but she did so only when prompted. Her parents were becoming increasingly discouraged, as they had hoped she would learn faster and communicate more. They knew the team was doing their best, and they worked hard to follow through at home, but Emily was not catching up, and some of her atypical and repetitive behaviors, such as spinning and rocking, were increasing.

At the end of her second preschool year, Emily's parents and educational team met and made a joint decision to seek an out-of-district placement, one in which she could get even more intensive services in a full-day, full-year program. Emily transitioned to a specialized school with a national reputation for its ABA program for children with autism spectrum disorders during her kindergarten year, and she spent the next several years there. She then transitioned to another autism school, also a reputable day program, and she has been there ever since. She is at school between 8 a.m. and 4 p.m. every day and then returns home. Both parents work full time, but they have organized their schedules so that one parent is always home when the bus drops her off.

Coping With the Present; Worried About the Future

Emily's younger sister is a third-grader in public school and also arrives home at the same time. The family doesn't have any child care
at home, but several relatives live close by, and they sometimes stop
by to spend a couple of hours with Emily, allowing her parents to
take a break and/or spend some time with their younger daughter.

Emily's family is happy with her educational placement. They
feel that the staff is very committed to her and really understand her
need for routine and predictability. Emily is calm, cheerful, and well
behaved most of the time; she always goes off to school willingly;
and she arrives home looking clean and "well put-together," as her
mother put it. "It's a good situation for Emily, but frankly, we are
exhausted and becoming increasingly worried. We adore Emily, but
we don't know what else we can do to prepare her for the future."

Step 2: Identify the Problem

Emily has an appropriate educational placement and a stable home
life. However, her progress in language and communication, social
skills, and daily living skills has been slow. Her parents report that
although her school team sends home a variety of different assignments and worksheets that she has allegedly completed or at least
participated in completing (very likely with a great deal of assistance), she does not do very much at home.

Reportedly, Emily is occupied during every minute of her
school day. She spends some time in her small classroom practicing picture communication. She has even learned to use some
communicative sounds and a few word approximations, and she
enjoys the time spent in the gross motor room. She especially likes
swinging, sliding, and jumping on the small trampoline. Once a
week she goes swimming, which is also a favorite activity. When
she arrives home, however, she has little to do, so she spends many

hours in front of the TV, usually watching the same two videos. Then she has dinner, her mother bathes her, and she goes to bed. By that time her parents are so tired themselves that they can barely find time to help Emily's sister with her homework or read with her or talk about her day before they fall asleep.

Emily's parents are quite aware and accepting of her limitations. They try to help her in every way they can, but they admit that they do a lot of things for her, maybe things she could learn to do for herself. They are wondering if she can learn a few routines. She has demonstrated the ability to, for example, get herself a snack and a drink. Her mother spent the better part of Saturday afternoon showing her how to make a peanut butter and jelly sandwich, and by the end of the day Emily was able to do so, albeit with considerable support, including verbal prompting and hand-over-hand assistance. However, she is not able to carry out most of her other daily living needs and requires a full assist for most of them. That is, she does not dress herself, bathe herself, take care of toileting or participate in doing any chores around the house, such as setting or clearing the table.

Both parents would like to see her learn to take on some of these responsibilities, and they have reason to believe that she will be able to, although it may take a great deal of training, supervision, and a lot of practice. Right now this is their primary goal.

Teaching Self-Help Routines

Emily's school team agrees that she should and very likely could learn certain skills and participate in household chores to a greater extent. At school, for example, she is able to get her own snack from the refrigerator, pour juice from a pitcher into a cup, and then gather her trash and throw it away. She does this along with several peers with whom she has snack and lunch daily. She is toilet trained, both at school and at home, but in both environments there is someone available to take her to the bathroom and help her with every step.

Emily's parents and school team admit that they have not pushed her to take on more responsibilities, but it is probably time to do so. Emily is only 15, and 22, the age at which her educational services cease, seems like it's a long way away, but, as her father says, "I can't believe how fast this first 15 years has gone. The time is flying by and we have to think about the future. What's next for Emily?"

Emily's school team would like to see her gain more independence, too. Although she can continue going to school until 22, she will transition to adult services at 18, and they need to have a plan in place before then. They know that it takes Emily a great deal of time to acquire skills, so this is the time to begin working on them. The more she is able to do for herself, the more options she will have in the future, in living arrangements, vocational placements, and/or adult programming.

In addition, Emily's parents and the school team would like to put together a program of activities that Emily could participate in outside of school. She has no social life, nor does she attend any groups or programs for adolescents with special needs. Her mother once tried a group at the "Y," but she never returned after the first meeting. She felt that Emily was the most impaired child there, and she was not really getting anything out of the group. She sat in the group for a few minutes, but she did not participate. Then she got up and spent the rest of the two-hour session looking out the window.

Emily's parents have tried to get her involved in other activities as well, but like the group at the "Y," they have often attended the first meeting or gone, for example, bowling or to the aquarium, and then never returned because of Emily's apparent indifference to everything they tried. They would like to figure out what kinds of activities she might enjoy and enroll her in some type of program, either after school or on weekends.

Step 3: State the Hypothesis, Yours and Others'

This is not an uncommon situation. Emily is going to a reputable school staffed by professionals who have a great deal of experience in working with students at various levels, including many who have similar and quite severe impairments like she does. Emily has some substantial strengths: Although she engages in some repetitive behaviors, like rocking and spinning, she is not self-injurious or generally disruptive. She functions well within her school setting, complies with requests most of the time, and follows a daily routine with a great deal of support. Although she has begun to take some responsibility, such as managing her own food, she has not really learned any additional daily living skills or increased independence. She is almost totally dependent on adult assistance and supervision.

At home, this is also the case. Emily's parents have not taught her to take care of her personal hygiene and many other daily living activities because, as they say almost apologetically, "She probably can do a lot more for herself, but honestly, it's so much easier to do most of it for her and get it done fast, and besides we're not sure how to teach her."

Working Toward Greater Independence

Emily's parents also recognize the reality of their situation. They are getting older, and they realize that Emily needs to learn some basic skills and routines, since they won't be around forever. Maybe they should have pushed her team to work harder on these skills, or they and their team should have worked more intensively with her at home. They've always prided themselves on taking care of her themselves, without asking for assistance, and they have never been comfortable with therapists, educators, and other providers coming and going from their home. But the fact is that they, alone, have not been able to teach her the tasks she needs to perform—and perhaps is capable of—including giving her multiple and ongoing opportunities to practice in order to cement those skills.

They also recognize that their younger daughter needs their attention. "We feel like she is raising herself, and we just check in once in a while," they say. And they have noticed that she is becoming increasingly resentful of her sister. While she loves Emily, she recently made comments to her parents, such as "I never have friends over. I always go to their houses. Pretty soon they are going to stop inviting me," and "I guess I'll never get married because I'll have to take care of her forever." That final statement gave her parents a real jolt.

The big question her parents and school team have is: Can Emily learn to follow at least some self-care routines? Both her parents and school team have hypothesized that she can, and both agree that they have not truly put in the intensive efforts and programming she needs to acquire these skills. With a major group effort, which will include some providers "coming and going" from their house, she may be able to learn some routines, which will give her some independence in the future and also contribute to a better quality of life for the rest of her family.

Seeking Out Recreational Activities

Another important issue is that Emily does need a life outside of school and home. Her parents have not had the opportunity to research the available options for leisure and recreational activities. The community based activities they have tried haven't been successful, and they are either too busy or too tired to keep searching and trying. Acquiring some self-care skills will also lead to more options for Emily in the community, but her family also needs assistance in identifying appropriate programs, getting her there and back, paying for them, and possibly providing adult support so that Emily can participate in a meaningful way. While they want Emily to enjoy recreational activities and develop some interests, they don't know what might appeal to her. They don't have any idea where to begin looking. It all seems like too much, like another full-time job. They felt that they could "manage" until now, but they know it's time to make some changes, for the good of the entire family.

Step 4: Review Treatment Approaches

Emily's school team, all of whom are very experienced in ABA, felt that there was no reason to consider radically different approaches to teaching her how to participate in more of her self-care and daily living skills. She had learned a few routines at school and could, at least, generalize them to her home environment. Emily's parents agreed, although they also wanted to see her improve communication and be able to do more independently. She is able to get an already-prepared snack, eat it, and throw away her trash, but she still requires prompting. She will cooperate with bathing and dressing but really isn't completing those tasks independently. The entire team agreed that beginning by teaching some simple daily living routines, at school and at home, would be the best place to start. And they would try to fast-track her. "Once she 'gets it,' we'll move to the next skill or routine immediately, rather than spending a lot of time congratulating her—and ourselves," the OT said, reassuringly.

Need for Generalization

In the past, Emily responded to programs that provided positive reinforcement through the use of edibles as well as playing with small, fidgety toys. The team had tried a token system, and although Emily routinely got enough tokens to trade in for preferred items or time playing with toys, she didn't really appear to understand the system. She was far more responsive when her behaviors were immediately reinforced, but simply reinforcing appropriate responses did not seem to be enough to cement, store, and then apply those skills elsewhere. Emily has never been able to consistently carry over learned skills from one setting to another. For example, at school, she is able to take her snack and lunch out of her lunchbox, open all the containers, eat with utensils, and then throw away her trash. At home, she does this once in a while, but not on a regular basis, and rarely without prompting. One of the differences is that at home, she is not required to do a lot for herself. She doesn't prepare meals or get her own food; she is simply asked to sit at the table with the family, and they all eat together.

Emily's mother recalls that Emily was very successful when she worked with her for several hours one day, making a peanut butter and jelly sandwich. She thought that teaching her in this manner would help her acquire similar skills. Emily's OT, who volunteered to head up the home-based training program, agreed. She dug up some research on an ABA approach that included task analysis, errorless learning, and backward chaining, which have been used successfully in teaching many students, including those who are very intellectually impaired, to learn new skills and complete various tasks (Jerome, Frantino, & Sturmey, 2007). A task analysis is a clear, detailed description of each activity needed to complete a task, including physical and cognitive requirements, duration and frequency of each step, and any environmental conditions necessary. Backward chaining involves breaking activities into small, very manageable skills, then working with an individual to teach each discrete task, moving backward from completion. For example, making a peanut butter and jelly sandwich would involve a trainer working with Emily, doing all the steps involved in making the sandwich, but leaving the last one out, which Emily would then do, first with hand-over-hand assistance, then with gestural or verbal prompting, and ultimately independently. This routine would continue, leaving the last two steps off and requiring Emily to do those, then the last three, and so forth, until she was able to complete all of the steps in the chain.

The rest of the team was aware of a large body of literature supporting backward chaining and related approaches (Frank, Wacker, Berg, & McMahon, 1985), and they shared it with Emily's parents. They felt that a similar approach would be successful in teaching Emily other self-help skills, including toileting and bathing, and possibly how to use a computer or play a simple board game.

As Emily has had some success over the years using very rudimentary picture communication, they also felt that simple, situation-specific picture schedules would help her in the bathroom, bedroom, and perhaps in other settings. Again, the team cited the literature supporting the use of the PECS system, even for students who have quite serious intellectual impairments (Charlop, Schreibman, & Thibodeau, 1985).

Emily's family was very much in favor of trying these interventions, but their concern was that they would not have enough time at home in order to work with her for the number of hours it might take to learn these routines. They recalled that when Emily was very young, they had several ABA trainers in and out of their house for many hours during the week, and Emily's mother admitted that it was very disruptive. They mentioned that Emily's sister would probably find it particularly annoying if Emily got even more attention. However, they agreed to try anything that would help Emily acquire more skills and independence for the sake of the entire family.

Community Resources

To begin the quest for helping Emily develop some leisure time interests and activities, Emily's family looked on the Internet and found several organizations that could possibly be helpful. They were not particularly concerned about what the literature said about which activities were better for children with autism; they simply wanted to identify activities that Emily could do and might enjoy, and organizations that would provide a safe environment for her and the adult support she would need.

They contacted their local autism support center, Easter Seals, and a local hospital that ran programs for families, including Sibshops®, which are activities-based support groups for the brothers and sisters of children with disabilities, created by Don Meyer (2007), parent groups, and mothers-only and fathers-only groups. They contacted their local ARC (formerly Association for Retarded Citizens), which is the largest national organization committed to supporting people with intellectual disabilities and their families. Through that process, they realized that there was a great deal of help available, but they just had not had the time or motivation to seek them out in the past. Now it was a priority.

Once they began researching the field, Emily's parents became a great deal more enthusiastic and motivated to pursue a variety of options for helping both their daughters and themselves. Her mother admitted, "We feel like we just kind of drifted through Emily's elementary and middle school years. Now that she is a real teenager, we need to teach her some skills and make some plans. This will be great for her and will also free us up. It will especially be good for Emily's sister." Emily's father added, "I didn't realize how many resources and how much good research was available out there, on just about everything. Not only are there dozens and dozens of academic studies on teaching the kids themselves, but there is plenty of research and lots of books and websites on the things that help families as a whole. This is really encouraging."

Step 5: Design the Treatment Plan

Emily's school team and parents got together to discuss the next steps. They decided to write a treatment plan that included both long- and short-term goals. They created what could be described as a modified "person-centered plan" (Amado & McBride, 2001; Kormann & Petronko, 2003). In many person-centered plans, the individual is encouraged to participate and express his or her needs and wishes, as well as how he or she might like to reach them. Emily had very little ability to do this, so her parents served as her "voice" and worked diligently to create a reasonable and viable plan, one that they thought Emily would make if she could. Their ultimate goal was to see Emily acquire the skills that she would need to live in a supported residence with others with similar needs and participate as much as she could in community life.

Toward that end, the team designed a plan for reaching short-term goals. These included doing task analyses and using backward chaining and other ABA techniques to teach her how to shower, be responsible for all her hygiene and toileting needs, choose her clothes, get herself dressed, and put away her personal items at home. The second tier of that plan would include teaching her more complex skills, such as food preparation and completing household chores, such as setting the table, putting away groceries, making her bed, and cleaning her room.

Recognizing Emily's parents' desires and the challenges they faced at home since they both worked and also needed to care for their younger daughter, the team agreed to (1) provide eight hours a week of home-based training that would include some parent training; (2) conduct a preference assessment in order to identify specific leisure and recreational activities that Emily could enjoy; (3) come up with a list of appropriate recreational programs, the requirements, schedule, and costs; and (4) identify other local and national agencies that could provide such services as respite care, transportation to and from activities, and help with any home alterations that might be necessary, such as structural or environmental modifications that would improve accessibility and safety. All team members realized that teaching Emily specific skills might take a great deal of time, but they all committed to participating. They agreed to shift the focus from a primarily school-based program to one that involved her family, her home, and connections to the community as a whole.

Step 6: Evaluate Effectiveness and Generate Your Own Evidence

During the first two months, Emily acquired some skills. She started off slowly and was somewhat resistant. That is not surprising, since she had not been pressured to work at such an intensive level either at home or at school. She was required to do many tasks that had previously been done for her. However, after doing a task analysis of bathing and toileting, and teaching her each step through backward chaining, she was able to complete both routines. Toileting proved to be a bit more difficult. She continues to get mixed up, doesn't always initiate, and still needs some adult support, but she is quite capable of taking her own showers, drying herself off, and getting dressed.

Certain environmental adjustments had to be made in order to help her become more successful. For example, Emily's parents got their plumbers to alter the faucets in the shower so that the water would never get too hot or too cold. They also clearly labeled all of her toiletries and glued pictures to them, such as her shampoo, conditioner, deodorant, and various lotions. Emily actually enjoyed going through these steps, taking more and more responsibility—and pleasure—in her personal grooming. She continues to need help with brushing and combing her hair, but her mother took her to get a stylish new haircut that was easier for her to care for herself. Emily easily mastered brushing her own teeth and putting coordinated outfits together through the use of situation-specific visual schedules in addition to modeling, videotaping, and teaching her how to complete each step. In every case, positive reinforcement was used, including more time to watch favorite videos and little treats, but most of the time, her family's enthusiasm and social praise were reward enough. She smiled frequently in response to their praise and immediately showed increased efforts.

It took another few months for Emily to learn how to make her bed, fold her clothes, and put away her personal belongings in her drawers and closets. Again, she was taught to follow simple picture schedules to complete many of the basic tasks. Labeling all of her drawers and cabinets in her bedroom has helped. Emily has been somewhat resistant to learning how to cook. She enjoys making sandwiches, microwaving popcorn, and arranging crackers and cheese, but she is not a big fan of measuring, mixing, or using multiple ingredients. However, her sister has begun to pitch in and actually enjoys cooking with her, especially when it involves baking cookies (Emily does well with premixed chocolate chip cookie dough) or making ice cream sundaes. Their mother said, "I walked into the kitchen one afternoon and there were my two girls, spraying canned whipped cream at each other, messing up the counters and floors and laughing uncontrollably. Maybe another mother would have been mortified. I couldn't have been more thrilled!"

Supported Participation

Through the local Autism Support Center, Emily's family was able to identify several groups for teenagers with autism. Emily attended a Friday night social, and although she did not actively participate in the dancing or karaoke, she sat on the side and happily watched, rocking to the music. With a great deal of support, she was also able to attend a group that painted ready-made pottery and plaster figures. Emily's mother reported that, "This is the first time I felt that she actually took pride in something she made. She brought home a plate she painted, gave it to me, and smiled." Emily's family tried several other activities, including a Challenger baseball league, a family-centered, national organization for children and adolescents with all kinds of disabilities, and a bowling group. Neither was especially successful. Emily seemed to get overwhelmed by all the noise and the crowd, which was not surprising. She's never been thrilled with team sports, but her parents wanted to try everything—and they aren't ruling out trying those activities again in the future. In fact, they made some connections through both activities with some families with children with disabilities who lived nearby. Her school social worker got her into an Easter Seals swim program that meets every Saturday morning, and she does enjoy that.

Emily's parents also met some families with teenagers with autism. They have never been big group joiners, but they liked the idea of remaining in touch with several families, by e-mail and occasionally by phone, in order to share information and resources, especially regarding future housing and living arrangements for their children.

Step 7: Redesign the Plan as Needed

Emily's parents and team had been changing and adjusting her program as they went along, but her parents decided to step up the pace on doing their own research into future housing options for Emily. They changed their policy to include looking at various "day hab" programs and supported residences earlier than planned. In the past, the team had begun this process when a student was about 18. However, they recognized the need to at least become familiar with what might be available when a student is younger, about 14 or 15, in order to make the best use of the years leading up to the transition to adult services.

Although the law in their state requires that a transitional plan should be put in place when a student turns 14, the specifics of that involvement are not well defined. So, most educational teams do not know what direction to take and end up having discussions about the future in the most general terms. By working very closely with Emily's family, her team got a better idea of where their efforts would be best spent. They knew it would take a long time—years, probably, to teach Emily skills that she could transfer, whether she ultimately was placed in a vocational setting or a day hab program.

At this point, her parents were more optimistic than they had been before. With hard work, consistency, and a constant examination and reordering of priorities, they saw Emily learn new skills, take on more responsibilities, and most important, enjoy a wider range of activities. They also saw many positive changes in every member of the family, now that they had a reasonable plan in place for Emily's future.

CHAPTER 10

CHEN: A TEENAGER WITH ASPERGER'S HITS BOTTOM, BUT WITH HELP AND DETERMINATION, HEADS FOR COLLEGE

"We've had so much support along the way, from school, friends, and all of our providers, and I really thought he was going to make it . . . until this year."

—Chen's mother

Step 1: Gather Background Information

Shortly after Chen, a 15-year-old who was diagnosed with Asperger syndrome in elementary school, transitioned to high school, his parents and the school team knew they needed to make a change in his program. He had done so well throughout his school years up to that point, or so it had seemed, but he had experienced a few traumas recently. His uncle, with whom he had been very close, died suddenly in a car accident when Chen was in eighth grade. Just being a 15-year-old boy was tough enough, with the biological changes and the increasingly complicated social scene.

It was a difficult year for the entire family, but by the end of the school year, Chen seemed to be thriving. He was getting good grades, and he appeared to be emotionally stable. By November of his freshman year, however, he began complaining about school and even refused to go several times. His grades began to decline, and his home life was becoming more stressful as well. He was showing increasing anger toward his parents around seemingly small issues, like when they had the bathroom floors retiled or gave away some old clothes that no longer fit him. Chen began spending more time at the computer, and he no longer got together with the few peers with whom he had always played video games.

Chen's parents came to the United States to pursue their careers in cancer research. They also thought it would be a better place to raise and educate Chen. Soon it became clear that he was bright, as he learned English very quickly once he was enrolled in school. He also continued to speak Chinese at home. However, his preschool teacher told his parents that he didn't play with the other children and that he almost never went to the pretend or dress-up areas.

Bright But Different

Initially, Chen's parents weren't overly concerned; they could see that he was a smart, kind, and happy boy who just seemed to have different interests from his peers. While they were playing fairies and pirates, he was drawing the solar system or studying the charts of animals and plants or flipping through the encyclopedia in the classroom. While they built cities out of blocks and Legos® or raced trucks and cars around the room, Chen did puzzles alone. Then, each afternoon when he got home from school, he loved to tell them about everything he had learned about his current topic of interest, which changed regularly, from the stars and planets to dinosaurs and volcanoes, and they listened appreciatively.

In elementary school, however, when Chen continued to spend most of his time alone and didn't play with other children, his parents began to worry. They brought up their concerns with his teacher, who said she told them this as well. She had noticed that at recess he was often alone, sometimes taking out paper and a pencil to do math problems, other times walking around the edge of the playground, talking to himself.

Chen's parents had read about Asperger syndrome and wondered if that might fit their son. They still weren't overly anxious, as one of their colleagues at work had announced he had Asperger's, and he was a very successful scientist. He was married with a baby on the way and was head of one of the research labs. Nevertheless, they took Chen to be evaluated by Dr. Woodlawn, a psychiatrist who came highly recommended by one of his colleagues, who confirmed their impression. The doctor was a bit surprised by their response: Chen's parents didn't appear devastated or even upset, as many parents are when they get such news. They actually seemed relieved. "So it's just what we thought," said Chen's father. "He is bright and sees the world a little differently than other children his age." "Yes, but how is he going to get by socially?" pointed out his mother. "He's doing well in school, but he doesn't have friends. Apart from one long term friendship, he's never even had a playdate. Not one." Dr. Woodlawn suggested they enroll him in a movie-making social skills group, since that was one of his interests. It might be easier for him to make friends with adult support in a group that didn't emphasize sports, but instead, was based on a common interest.

Focus on Social Skills

Chen's parents shared Dr. Woodlawn's report with the school and asked that they provide some help with his social skills. He attended regular classes with pull-out services twice a week for social skills group instruction. He had enrolled in the movie-making social skills group outside of school, too, and he loved it.

As he grew, he went through periods of passionate interests in topics and activities, starting with Pokémon™ and evolving to ancient history, Legos®, cars, mythology, geography, geology, physics, computer games, and making Claymation movies. He finally made friends with a classmate in third grade, which lasted until eighth grade, when that child became increasingly involved in team sports and his teammates, and the two spent less time together. Up to that point, the other child shared Chen's many passions. The two could play for hours together and gradually created increasingly complex movies and did science experiments. Chen's parents hoped this special friendship would continue. It made Chen so happy and brought out the best in him. Chen's parents even imagined that they might go into the film production business together someday.

Chen's uncle was similar to Chen, and the two developed a close bond. He and Chen also worked on complicated science projects together, went to museums, the zoo, and for long walks. When Chen's uncle died unexpectedly in a car accident, the whole family was thrown into turmoil. Not only was it a loss for them, but they also knew that he was a beloved friend and mentor and a key figure in Chen's life. Chen was grief stricken and became practically despondent.

Impact of Loss

Chen lost interest in his former passions. He complained about school, often claimed he "had a headache" and couldn't go, and he avoided going anywhere in the car. He was also becoming increasingly irritable at home, responding rudely if his parents asked him to do simple chores, like clearing the table or taking out the trash—chores he used to do on his own—and he snapped at them if they asked him about his day. His parents sought out the guidance of Dr. Woodlawn, the psychiatrist who originally diagnosed him. He thought that Chen was probably depressed, which was not surprising given his strong attachment to his uncle, and he suggested therapy to help Chen through it. Dr. Woodlawn explained that depression can show up in children as sadness and loss of interest in former enjoyable activities with adults, but it can also manifest as irritability, just as they were seeing at home, and a decline in academic performance, as they were seeing at school (Ward, Sylva, & Gresham, 2010).

Cognitive-Behavioral Therapy May Help With Anxiety

So Dr. Woodlawn referred Chen to a therapist, a social worker who specialized in therapy for teenagers with Asperger's and also had a background in grief counseling. Chen participated in this therapy weekly for six months and showed major improvements. This therapist used Cognitive-Behavioral Therapy (CBT) to treat what had become a real phobia of car travel as well as more tradition talk therapy to help Chen with grief and loss issues. She also worked with his parents, giving the family homework in practicing CBT techniques regularly to help Chen conquer his fear of car travel.

By the end of eighth grade, Chen seemed to be his old cheerful self. He began pursuing his interests again, although he deeply missed both his uncle and his former best friend. He began attending school again, happily, and returned to his movie-making social group. He quickly mastered a new complicated film editing program with many professional features and spent many hours at home on his computer, editing movies he had worked on with his group. He was no longer afraid of cars, and he was rarely irritable at home anymore.

Over the summer after his eighth-grade year, however, Chen became very anxious about starting high school. He worried about everything, from the large size of the school to the noisy and crowded hallways to the complexities of the social world that was already too challenging for him in middle school. He also worried about all of the courses he would have to take, the homework, and the exams.

His parents didn't understand this, as he had done well in all his subjects for much of his school life, but Chen told them, "I've heard it gets a lot harder, especially English and Social Studies." Besides, he was beginning to find those subjects more difficult in eighth grade. He wondered if he was "just stupid," because he often had no idea when the English teacher would ask specific questions, like why characters acted the way they did, or what he thought was going to happen next in a story. He noticed that his classmates, even the ones who fooled around a lot in class, seemed to have the answers, as if it were simple, even obvious.

In September, Chen began high school with trepidation. He went to all of his classes and did his homework, but his parents noticed he was much more serious, somewhat lethargic, and unhappy. He again started complaining about going to school, saying his stomach or head hurt. His first-term grades included some C's and a D in English. This was a sharp contrast to his grades in the past: mostly A's with a couple of B's. He continued to get A's in math and science, however.

Although he certainly wasn't as happy, Chen did develop an interest in computer programming, and he taught himself how to use several complicated systems. As usual, his parents supported his interests. They had a friend who did "App" development, who they connected with Chen. So when he wasn't in school, Chen enjoyed working on projects with the family friend and soon began to develop an original app on his own.

Step 2: Identify the Problem

Chen's parents were encouraged by his new interests, but they and Chen's school team scheduled a meeting to discuss their mutual concerns about his dropping grades. Chen's parents were also concerned that he might be depressed again, and they wondered about taking him back to his old therapist. Chen had told his parents that he also wanted to attend the team meeting, since he had never attended one, and everyone agreed that would be helpful. He was 15, and the special education laws in his state explicitly stated that students can attend their team meetings beginning at age 14.

Learning About Learning Disabilities

At the meeting, Chen told the team that English language arts was especially hard for him. His teacher noted that he seemed to have the most difficulty with abstract assignments and also organizing the steps for longer-term projects in English, but in other subjects. They wondered if he might have a learning disability, even though he was obviously very bright. One teacher speculated that maybe he had been compensating when he was younger, but as the pace and complexity were increasing, he was no longer able keep up.

Chen listened carefully, and he recalled that some of the work seemed far more difficult. He wondered if he might "be getting dumber," since he was spending hours and hours on assignments, rather than racing through them as he did in middle school. The school psychologist explained the concept of a learning disability—that it didn't mean that he was "dumb," but rather, that he processed information in a different way, and that was reassuring to Chen and his parents.

Sensory Sensitivities

Chen then expressed how bothered he was by the very crowded, noisy hallways between classes, and that he spent the end of each class worrying about getting to his locker and making his way to the next class on time. He also said that the cafeteria crowds bothered him, and he was rarely able to eat lunch.

The principal pointed out that with construction going on in a nearby town, the school had far more students than usual. Chen wondered if he might leave class a little early to get to his next class before the crowds filled the halls. The team agreed they would try that for now, but that could become confusing if Chen missed key assignments or other information at the end of each period. The occupational therapist agreed to meet with Chen to further explore and identify what, specifically, about this situation bothered him and develop a treatment plan to reduce his distress.

Chen also told the team that he sometimes found school and homework getting in the way of his computer programming, which he loved. Because he knew he wanted to do this as his career, he asked why he needed to "learn all that other stuff like literature and current events." He thought he would do better if he were allowed to specialize in his interest now, rather than waiting until college, which was years away.

Chen's parents expressed their ongoing concerns about his having no friends, especially since his best friend was no longer spending time with him. Chen said he wanted more friends, too.

So the team identified the problems as follows:

- Chen's declining grades and his own growing distress about his academic struggles
- Chen's anxiety about the crowds between classes and in the cafeteria
- Chen's wanting more friends
- Chen requested that the team to be sure to add that he wasn't able to spend enough time on computer programming and had to learn about subjects in which he had no interest.

Step 3: State the Hypothesis, Yours and Others'

In order to explore various hypotheses around these problems, the following steps were taken. Chen's parents scheduled a neuropsychological assessment to explore the possibility of a learning disability, which might explain his dropping grades. Chen would meet with the occupational therapist, who would administer a sensory integration assessment. The resulting sensory profile might point to one or more sensory components during class changes and other transtions that were aversive to him. The OT had worked with many students with autism spectrum disorders and other disabilities, and she knew that those with sensory integration dysfunction often find crowded, noisy, fast-paced, or chaotic environments highly uncomfortable.

Chen and his parents also discussed returning to the therapist who had helped him in the past, so she could evaluate him for depression and determine if that was contributing to his lowered grades. Perhaps his social isolation was the cause of—or a contributing factor to—his academic difficulties. Chen and his parents also wondered if she could use the CBT techniques that had previously helped him overcome his car phobia, to help him with what was becoming a crowded hallway phobia.

Although Chen and his parents were concerned about his social isolation, his school team hadn't been as aware of this situation and so hadn't identified this as a major problem. Chen expressed his wish to spend more time working at the computer and less time in other classes. He speculated that this could also be contributing to his dropping grades.

Step 4: Review Treatment Approaches

Chen was evaluated by a neuropsychologist, who shared her findings with Chen and the team. She found that he was extraordinarily gifted in several areas, especially math, and also functioned in the superior range in some aspects of memory. She was not surprised at his talent and interest in computer programming. She also identified difficulties in executive functioning, especially time management and organization, as well as challenges with abstraction and inference. There were large discrepancies in his skills in comparison with his peers, with some abilities approaching college level and others that were substantially below grade/age level. She explained that this learning profile/learning disability pattern, while not typical in the larger, general learning disability population, is common in individuals with Asperger's disorder (Ryburn, Anderson, & Wales, 2011).

Processing Problems

The neuropsychology evaluation also uncovered some other interesting learning challenges, including deficits in processing language at a rapid pace. This may be contributing to Chen's difficulty in learning in a large-class lecture format, which was common in his high school. In contrast, middle-school classes had been smaller and included more hands-on learning, so it wasn't surprising that his learning problems hadn't surfaced before high school. Chen was relieved to know he wasn't "getting dumber," and he gained a better understanding of how he learned. He became interested in the brain and asked to meet with the neuropsychologist regularly, because he wanted to understand more. She didn't have time but referred him to the lab of one of her colleagues, who did neurocognitive research and was willing to meet with him.

Chen's former therapist met with him for three sessions. She felt that Chen was again becoming depressed, as a result of his social isolation and school difficulties. Both issues—social isolation and school failure—can lead to depression (Ward, Sylva, & Gresham, 2012) and is a very common pattern and cause of depression in teens with Asperger's (Whitehouseet al., 2009). She agreed with Chen that more time doing what he was interested in would probably be helpful, but that he also needed more help with developing friendships. She agreed to attend the next team meeting.

Chen and his therapist also explored his difficulties with the crowding at school. She asked if there were times when this did not bother him, and he said that when he was walking with his math teacher from class on the third floor to the cafeteria, they talked about math and he didn't notice the crowds as much. However, once he was in the cafeteria, it bothered him a lot. He talked about being preoccupied and worried, especially at the end of every class and before lunch. His therapist felt he was vulnerable to anxiety, and that this could be treated with CBT since he had responded so well before.

The occupational therapist went through a sensory profile questionnaire with Chen, which revealed that crowded, noisy, and/or chaotic environments caused him to become anxious. It wasn't clear how much of this was based on the social confusion and how much was purely sensory overload. Nevertheless, crowds bothered him. Further discussions revealed that Chen found listening to classical music to be extremely calming.

Step 5: Design the Treatment Plan

The team convened to design a plan, now that they had reviewed the results and recommendations of all of the specialists who had been involved in this assessment process. Chen attended this meeting, too. They worked out the following plan together:

1. *Chen would receive learning disability support for the classes in which he was having difficulty.* A specialist on staff taught smaller, more individualized classes in these subjects. He would continue to take advanced math and science but would move to the LD classes for his other subjects. Chen's parents were concerned this might limit his options for college, but the team reassured them that many students with a similar profile graduated high school and went on to college, and that a growing number of colleges had learning supports on campus.

2. *Chen's therapist would work with him and the school psychologist to develop a plan based on CBT techniques to help him learn to tolerate the crowded hallways and other overstimulating environments.* His math teacher had volunteered to walk with him between some classes, although he wasn't always available.

3. *Chen could choose to have lunch in the computer lab with a few other students who also had difficulty with noise and crowds.* Chen's parents worried that this would isolate him further, but Chen pointed out that he didn't talk to anyone at lunch anyway. At least he would be able to relax and eat in the computer lab. Chen's parents asked if a computer teacher, or a paraprofessional with computer expertise and ideally with social skills training, could also eat with the students in the computer lab and make this a social-computer lunch club. The school agreed to look into this option.

4. *The school team proposed that Chen participate in the school's social skills group for students with autism.* Chen's parents knew some of these children from their connections in the local autism community and felt that Chen's social difficulties were quite different from theirs. Most of these children had significant cognitive impairments, were far less verbal, and were not as socially skilled as Chen. They proposed that the school fund his participation in a drama program for teens with Asperger's that met on Saturdays, as well as a vacation camp and two summer sessions. There was some discussion about whether there was any evidence supporting this approach, and the school psychologist found that there were several studies that provided evidence (e.g., Lerner, Mikami, & Levine, 2000). The school team still felt uneasy as evidence was limited. However, Chen's therapist had read up on social skills groups, including Michelle Garcia Winner's book *A Politically Incorrect Look at Evidence-Based Practices and Teaching Social Skills (2002),* and discovered no one social skills approach was supported by a large body of evidence.

5. *Chen again brought up his interest in spending more time on programming and especially app development.* The family friend who was coaching him, it turned out, was looking for an entry

level assistant, and his family agreed Chen could work for him two afternoons per week and a few hours on the weekend. Their friend also had some college students working with him, so there might also be opportunities to find some friends, or at least make contact with people with similar interests. Chen's parents also reasoned that this would be a good activity to add to his college applications when the time came.

The team agreed to put this plan into place and work toward achieving the following goals in the next three months:

1. Chen would earn B's or above in his LD classes.
2. Chen would work with the school psychologist on the plan based on CBT for increasing his comfort level between classes, in addition to transitioning with the math teacher for two of his classes.
3. At the OT's suggestion, Chen could listen to classical music on his iPod as he went from class to class. At first the team objected, saying this would limit his social opportunities, but Chen immediately pointed out that he didn't ever interact with anyone in the halls between classes, as he was putting all his energy into "just surviving." This made sense; when people are anxious, they are less likely to engage in new or challenging activities or take social risks.
4. Chen would eat lunch in the computer lab with peers and with one of the computer teachers, who had agreed to create challenging computer activities, problems, and brain-teasers for the students to tackle together as a group as they ate.
5. The school would fund Chen's participation in the drama-based social group for one term and determine if he had made gains in forming friendships in or outside of school or if he was finding it easier to participate in social situations or "read" his peers' verbal and nonverbal cues.

6. Chen had learned online about a support group for teens with Asperger's and asked his parents if he could join.

Step 6: Evaluate Effectiveness and Generate Your Own Evidence

The team put the plan in place and reconvened in three months. The results were largely positive. Chen had grown more comfortable in the hallways through regular practice with CBT techniques. He became more relaxed and confident because he knew he would be having lunch in the computer room, rather than in the cafeteria, which reduced his anxiety considerably. Knowing that his math teacher would be with him for some of the transitions also reduced his anxiety. Using his iPod to listen to music also helped him stay calm.

Making Friends Makes a Difference

Chen enjoyed his drama social skills program and had made two friends there. They shared his interest in computer programming, too. He had gotten together with them several times outside of the program, taking turns meeting at each other's houses.

Two concerns remained:

1. *Chen did not like his learning disability classes even though he was getting B's in both.* He said they were "boring" and that the other students did not seem interested, either. He also said some of the other students rolled their eyes and even laughed when he volunteered an answer, which didn't happen in his other classes, and he thought they thought he was strange or dumb or both.
2. *Chen still did not have any friends at school, although he had made friends both in his drama group and at his computer job.* He and his parents felt it was much easier for him to make friends with teenagers with whom he shared a common interest.

Step 7: Redesign the Plan as Needed

The computer lunch group, which had sounded promising, wasn't working out. It wasn't functioning as a group, because the other students weren't as interested in computers and talked more about sports and the social scene at school. Chen had little interest in these topics and didn't participate in those discussions. So although it got him out of the cafeteria, it wasn't helping him form friendships.

The principal looked further into the difficulties in Chen's learning disability class. While in past years these had been small, dynamic, hands-on classes, taking on students from the high school under construction changed the makeup of the classes, both in size and approach to teaching. Students with a variety of reasons for failing regular classes had been placed in these classes, so they were busier, noisier, and presented more challenges for the teachers and students.

Considering Educational Options

Chen had heard about a school in his Asperger support group that was especially for teenagers with Asperger's who were bright and didn't have behavior problems, and who planned to go to college—students like him. He had heard that the classes were small and designed for students with his learning strengths and weaknesses. He looked it up online and it was very expensive, but it looked just right for him. This would help him learn better, prepare him for college, help him have more friends, and get him out of his boring learning disability classes, he thought. He brought it up with his parents, and they brought it up with the school team. The team said they understood the parents' concerns, but as he was making gains in all areas and they were funding the social skills group outside of school, they didn't plan to recommend this other program as it would be more restrictive and limit his interactions with typical peers.

Chen and his parents decided to visit the private school anyway. After the visit, Chen commented, "I think they must have known all about me when they created this school." His parents agreed. They saw how in the small classes social interaction was more naturally taking place, as students discussed and argued about topics that interested them. They also noticed how skilled the teachers were in facilitating interactions and getting the students to cooperate, collaborate, and problem solve.

They saw students who reminded them of Chen chatting and laughing with peers in the hallways. The lunchroom was carpeted and quiet, and students ate at small, family-style tables. Furthermore, they learned that 80% of the students who graduated attended college. They knew their options were to try to convince their school team that this was a better fit for Chen and get the district's support or to pay the tuition themselves.

They appreciated the many efforts the school had made to help Chen; they felt he had made important gains; and they liked and trusted his team. But they were concerned about his continued isolation and the limited success the school had had in addressing his learning disability and social needs. They didn't yet know which route they were going to take, but they left the school tour determined that their son would succeed and go on to college.

CHAPTER 11

MICHAEL: A 10-YEAR-OLD WHOSE BEHAVIORS ARE BECOMING MORE DISRUPTIVE AND AGGRESSIVE

"I can't sleep at night worrying that he might hurt the baby or me. He's such a sweet little boy. I know he can't help himself, but he's getting bigger and stronger and I don't know what we are going to do."

—Michael's mother

"He behaves at my house when I'm there but not with the baby-sitter, and I can't be there all the time. Besides, when he's with his mother, she can't control him."

—Michael's father

Step 1: Gather Background Information

Michael is a 10-year-old boy with a diagnosis of autistic disorder and an intellectual disability. Recent testing results indicate he functions more like a 2-year-old in many areas. He doesn't have any verbal language but signs "more" and "all done" and understands concrete choice questions, especially related to his favorite activities. He has an iPad, which he uses primarily for playing spelling games and watching favorite videos. Sometimes he uses a voice output picture based program on it for requesting at school, but not at home. Michael is a very active and impulsive child. He has an additional diagnosis of ADHD.

Michael's parents, Paul and Lauren, now separated, recall that he was an easy baby, at least for the first year. But they sensed that something wasn't right, shortly after his first birthday. He started to walk around that time, right on schedule, but then began running back and forth in the kitchen, repeating the same pattern, from the stove to the pantry to the refrigerator, over and over. "I think he would have done this for hours if we didn't stop him," added Lauren. Both Paul and Lauren also noticed that while he occasionally smiled, he rarely smiled directly at them, and he didn't respond to his name. Michael continued to run in patterns and started to open every door and cabinet he spotted. Although his parents knew toddlers liked to do this, there was an unusual quality to his actions. Michael would run to the oven, open and close it several times, then run to the opposite end of the kitchen, open and close the pantry door several times, and then run to the refrigerator. He became so obsessive that his parents soon put childproof locks on everything.

Behaviors Escalate

As Michael got a little older, his behaviors became more challenging. He began darting out the front door whenever his mother stepped out to pick up the mail—or for any other reason. He soon learned to unlock and open it himself. Paul changed the locks on all of the doors, placing them above his reach. Not discouraged by this obstacle, Michael soon learned to push a chair to the door, climb on it, and open it. He was able to unlock and open both the front and back doors, the door to the basement, and the one leading to the garage. "There was no safe place," Paul remembers.

Other unusual behaviors surfaced. One day, Lauren was cooking and Michael was in the adjoining dining room, happily playing, or so she thought. She went in and found him standing on the table, stark naked, slipping and sliding in a pile of salt and oil he had dumped on the table. Another day, Paul walked into the kitchen and found that Michael had dumped out an entire gallon of milk and was "painting" everything—the walls, the floors, the cabinets, and himself!

Paul and Lauren soon stopped going to family get-togethers, as it became a constant battle just to keep him safe. Michael didn't sleep well either, and Lauren and Paul were exhausted and irritable all the time. He woke up several times a night, almost every night, and easily learned to climb out of his crib. His pediatrician recommended a safe crib topping, but they weren't comfortable "putting a lid on him," so they put his mattress on the floor and placed yet another childproof lock on his door, since he had easily learned to scale every safety gate they tried. Lauren or Paul would quietly peek in at night or in the morning, dreading what they would find; he often took off his clothes, had had bowel movements, and spread it around the room.

Exhaustion Increases Stress

Lauren and Paul were completely exhausted, stressed in every way, and worse, they were growing very worried. Lauren especially felt hopeless, isolated, and depressed, as she was home with Michael most of the time. Paul began spending more time at work and announced that he had to begin traveling more for his job as a marketing manager for a small company, but Lauren suspected that at least part of the reason was that he simply dreaded coming home.

Despite all of these very challenging behaviors, Michael was a very endearing child. He went to his parents for hugs and cuddles, climbed up onto their laps, and began smiling more, especially when they praised him. He loved swinging and running around outside and would shriek with pleasure when his father chased or roughhoused with him. He also loved music and could find his favorite songs on YouTube and through other iPad apps. He was very curious and very mechanically adept.

Seeking Out Home-Based Behavioral Help

Shortly before Michael began preschool, Lauren and Paul split up. They remained on good terms and were united in their devotion to Michael. They both were pleased with his program, as he began making gains behaviorally, but he continued to need one-on-one support. At his mother's house, he needed constant supervision, and she sought the help of Kerry, a behavioral specialist, who was recommended by Michael's preschool teacher. After the initial intake, Kerry visited each parent's house for an hour each week to provide guidance and coach them on how to handle specific problems. Kerry recommended bolting down all movable furniture, added "Houdini-proof" locks, as she called them, and created a truly childproof playroom out of the guestroom at his mother's house, where he spent the majority of his time.

Kerry also showed both parents how she could get Michael to come back to her without unintentionally reinforcing his escape attempts by appearing to panic or making it into a fun game of chase. However, several challenging situations came up weekly. Michael still managed to get out of his mother's house and would run into the street, so she had to chase him to keep him safe. A few times he pushed right past her and ran to the end of the block before she caught up with him, completely out of breath. Another time he was so intent on getting out of the house that he had pushed her over as she was blocking the door. Michael was getting bigger and stronger, and Lauren was worried. Michael was a little easier to manage at his father's house. Paul was a relatively large, strong man, and he was usually able to stop Michael before he could escape.

Kerry felt that both parents followed the behavior plan extremely well, but that Lauren was not always able to prevent him from getting out of the house. He would be calm and cooperative for a couple of weeks and then, without warning, figure out a new way to escape, so his unpredictability was making life very difficult.

Finally, a Diagnosis

By age 4, Michael still hadn't begun to talk, so his parents scheduled a full developmental evaluation. He was diagnosed with autism, intellectual disability, and ADHD. Lauren and Paul were very upset, especially about the autism diagnosis, because they worried about how that label might define him for the rest of his life, They also knew it would lead to getting some help for their child. They enrolled him in their public school program for children with autism spectrum disorders, and he began receiving home-based help for his behavioral challenges. The doctor who assessed him, an autism specialist with whom they had developed a good rapport and a great deal of trust, also suggested they might try medication to help with his impulsivity and sleep, which they agreed to. The added support, school, and medication all seemed to help, and life became a bit easier.

Michael continued to attend the public school's full-day autism program. By the time he was eight, he had not learned to communicate using the Picture Exchange Communication System (PECS) that is often helpful for nonverbal children. He held the pictures and flipped and flicked them by his eyes, but if they were on a table or board, he showed no interest in them. He used a few signs, but he mostly communicated by pushing an adult to what he needed. He had learned some more self-regulation and was able to, with a staff person by his side at all times, stay in the classroom most of the time and do some simple tabletop work, like stacking blocks, matching pictures, and imitating visual patterns. He continued to need one-on-one support throughout the school day; when there was a gap in staffing, he would often run out of the room, down the hall, and in and out of other classrooms. Twice he had gotten out of the building. He had become "schedule toilet trained" at school and was able to help with dressing, undressing, and handwashing, with prompting, but he hadn't learned to complete any of those tasks independently.

Over the next year, challenges at home continued, with little improvement. Michael had the most difficulty, both at home and at school, on "change days," when he was transitioning from one parent's home to the other. But both parents agreed that there were no easy days, just days that weren't quite as hard. Although he was slowly learning self-help skills at school, he was not generalizing outside of school. His parents brought him to the bathroom on schedule since he didn't initiate, and they prompted him through each step. He often objected, would scream, and sometimes throw things or hit himself. His parents had become so discouraged and frustrated that they became less consistent about taking him to the bathroom or going through his self-care routine.

Step 2: Identify the Problem

Both of Michael's parents were feeling completely exhausted, overwhelmed, and increasingly worried that they would not be able to keep him safe at either home. Lauren had by now remarried and had a new baby. She was also worried that Michael might accidentally hurt the baby, as he still had no safety awareness, especially when he was intent on getting something he wanted. He had hurt his mother on several occasions while trying to leave the house. Paul continued to have more success at his house, but he worked long hours and relied on babysitters, some of whom were skilled and some who weren't. At least two had quit without warning, saying that Michael was too difficult to handle. Both homes had furniture bolted to the floors and walls. Neither parent felt comfortable going out in the community with him unless they had two adults along and no other children, and neither parent entertained at home. So Michael spent most of his time outside of school, alone, in his playroom or bedroom.

Slow Progress

Both parents were also concerned that his progress was so slow. He had been in school for several years now and only knew a few signs. He wasn't toilet trained and didn't have other independent self-care skills. He still liked the same few activities he had always liked and hadn't taken any interest in new toys or people.

Michael's school staff felt he was making progress. He rarely tried to escape the classroom, although he had one-on-one support at all times. They reported that he was able to focus and complete some tasks. For example, he had learned five colors and most of the letters of the alphabet receptively, and he could assemble letters to spell his name. He was showing some interest in putting together floor-size 8-to 10-piece puzzles. While his parents were pleased that he was doing better at school, they agreed that the primary problems were safety and lack of generalization and limited progress.

At school there was a consistently high teacher-to-student ratio, a well-trained and experienced staff, and a predictable routine. So understandably, the school did not view safety as a major concern. The staff also felt that Michael was making progress in behavior and self-care, although they too were concerned about his very slow communication progress and lack of initiating self-care routines.

At the next Individualized Education Plan (IEP) meeting, Michael's parents brought up the subject of residential schools for the first time, saying that they wanted to at least explore the possibilities. They both loved him very much, and it was painful for them to even consider this as an option, but they both felt that Michael's life at home was unsafe and very limited. Furthermore, both parents were finding themselves becoming increasingly depressed, agreeing, "We all feel like prisoners. This isn't fair to Michael and it isn't fair to us."

Michael's parents and school team agreed that more behavioral support at home would be added to his IEP. They agreed to bring in the behavioral experts from one of the top residential schools in the area. The social worker on the school team was also going to help the family look into ways to get more behavioral support at home from state and local agencies. The family agreed to this with the stipulation that they would reconvene the team after three months of home behavioral support to determine if there had been any improvements. The team identified and agreed on a set of specific goals to work toward and evaluate at the end of that period. These would be key in determining whether Michael could continue to live at home. These included the following:

- He would not bolt out of the house if the door was unlocked.
- He would not show any aggression toward his mother for a month.
- He would not throw any heavy objects or furniture for a month.
- He would be able to go out with the family to gatherings and community locales, such as the park or a restaurant, without needing to be restrained or removed.

Regarding Michael's lack of progress in ADLs at home, the behavior support team, including school staff and outside providers, agreed to work directly on these skills at home with these agreed-upon goals:

- He would become independent for toileting, with reminders.
- He would dress and undress himself, with decreasing amounts of support.

Regarding lack of progress in communication, the team agreed to an evaluation by an Augmentative and Alternative Speech and Language Communication (AAC) specialist.

Step 3: State the Hypothesis, Yours and Others'

The school team and both parents felt that the combination of Michael's high activity level, difficulty inhibiting his actions, and cognitive delays contributed to most of his challenges. However, nobody really understood why he was so intent on bolting out the door or why he threw furniture. Lauren, Paul, and the school team speculated that the transitions across homes added a level of difficulty for him, but they weren't sure how to make those transitions easier. They also agreed that he wasn't able to generalize and so was unsuccessful in toileting at his parents' homes and that he needed to be taught in each environment. It wasn't clear to anyone why he wasn't making more progress in communication. He certainly seemed like he wanted to communicate.

The behavioral specialist brought in from the residential school conducted a Functional Behavioral Assessment (FBA). She observed on several occasions and at different times at each parent's home and at school. She interviewed family members and school staff. Her job was easier than is often the case, since all parties agreed about most of the behaviors.

Her initial report indicated that Michael was motivated to get outside because he loved to run, and even with consistent blocking of access, he still made efforts to leave the house. It was easier to get out at his mother's house, since she wasn't as strong or as able to block him. She felt the behavior plan the school had set up and the parents were trying to carry out was quite sound. The challenge was to figure out what was driving his other maladaptive behaviors and what else could be done to help him.

Impulsivity Hard to Control

As external measures hadn't been sufficient to help with his impulsivity, the behavioral specialist wondered about an underlying biological cause of his impulsivity and if this was strong enough to override even the best behavior plan. She consulted with his occupational therapist, and they explored the possibility of his need for more sensory input and considered whether a sensory diet might be helpful. Perhaps scheduling periods of swinging and jumping, adding deep pressure massages, or trying to teach him very basic breathing exercises would help. She also wondered about the degree to which his communication challenges were contributing to his frustrations. Maybe he would try to bolt less if he had a way to ask to go out and run—or for anything else he wanted.

Furthermore, maybe teaching him communication directly related to his behaviors might help motivate him to communicate more in general. She looked forward to the recommendations of his upcoming augmentative communication assessment. Finally, she wondered, as did his parents, if he really understood his schedule, especially the process of switching homes. That is, did he know when to expect which parent? Did he know where he was going when he was picked up? She explained that predictability could greatly reduce his behavior challenges.

Despite all the additional help and some new insights, the family was becoming increasingly exhausted and even more discouraged. The behaviorist was familiar with the large body of research indicating the many different ways intensive caregiving takes a toll on the health and well-being of caregivers (Sloper & Beresford, 2006). She was also familiar with the literature from multiple fields indicating that having exhausted, discouraged, or depressed parents can also lead to increased mood and behavioral problems in children, as well as parents finding it more difficult to consistently follow through with communication or behavioral plans (Downey & Coyne, 1990; Rutter, 1990). Perhaps their exhaustion was greater than anyone realized, and they needed more emotional support. This, too, may have been a factor that was playing a role in Michael's behavior.

Step 4: Review Research

At the behaviorist's suggestion, the family was willing to take Michael to a neurologist who specialized in treating complicated children with developmental and behavioral challenges, to explore whether medication could be useful for his impulsive behaviors that hadn't responded so far to more traditional behavioral interventions. The neurologist felt that because behavioral approaches had been tried, it could be useful to start a trial of medication to treat his hyperactivity and impulsivity. As it would be about a month before the new behavioral plan and supports would be in place, this could provide enough time to evaluate the medication's effectiveness. He gave the family and school checklists and instructed them to keep daily records of behaviors he identified as likely to decrease in response to the medication, as well as possible side effects to look for.

The behaviorist accompanied the family to the AAC assessment. The speech and language pathologist (AAC-SLP) specialist tried out a simple new program on her iPad with Michael. She showed him how to touch a photograph of what he wanted, and the iPad "spoke" the word. Then he was given the object immediately. While he hadn't shown much interest in the Picture Exchange Communication System (PECS), he responded more enthusiastically to this program, quickly learning to request items with this voice output system. She worked with his family and the behaviorist to come up with vocabulary that would be most important and motivating for him. These included photographs of the outside places he liked to run: his backyard at each house and the school playground, as well as some other favorite activities, like the puzzle he had learned to assemble and a set of plastic letters. His parents asked what to do if he requested something he couldn't have. What if he woke up in the middle of the night and requested "backyard"? Did this mean they had to bring him outside? The AAC-SLP and behaviorist assured them they did not have to give him everything he asked for! They were advised to try to take him out as often as possible when he requested it at appropriate times. When he, like any child, begins to learn to request, they should always respond by acknowledging his request. However, he also needs to learn that making a request does not always lead to having the request met.

The behaviorist then suggested a picture schedule, and the AAC-SLP had an "app" in which photographs could be inserted into a schedule. This schedule would be easily accessible, and it could be easily changed. It could prove to be useful at both houses and at school, to ease transitions and also to provide an enjoyable activity that he could do with all of the key people in his life.

The occupational therapist summarized for the team some of the research on sensory diets for children with high activity levels, impulsivity, and autism, which she had obtained at a recent conference, and all agreed that this component should be included in his plan, too.

Step 5: Design the Treatment Plan

The consulting behaviorist worked with the team to revise Michael's behavior plan to include the following:

1. With consultation from the occupational therapist, a sensory diet would be implemented, which would include

time to run around outside with one of his favorite staff people when he arrives at school, at mid-day, and before going home. Playing chase and completing obstacle courses were also included in the plan to foster his social and regulatory goals while he expended energy and engaged in this highly preferred activity. She also made a similar plan for home.

2. With the recommendations from the AAC-SLP, a plan was designed for using his communication system to request time to play outside and favorite people, foods, and other activities. The family had an iPad that could accommodate this system.

3. To help with transitions, the AAC-SLP would teach the family and school staff how to create situation-specific picture schedules for use throughout his day. She would also coach them on using pictures and language so he could anticipate who was going to pick him up, which house he was going to after school, and any other future events.

4. The behaviorist introduced her two paraprofessionals to the family for their work at home. They all met to develop steps to reaching the goals identified in each home regarding safety, communication, self-care, and behaviors on community outings.

5. In addition to putting in place the home-based program, the social worker would help the family establish eligibility for center-based respite care two weekends each month, including one overnight per weekend.

6. A special parent support group was identified in the area, which focused on the needs of children with more severe autism symptomology, as well as their parents' needs. Michael's mother had also decided to find her own therapist. His father said he would think about this option for sometime in the future.

7. Data would be taken at home and at school on behaviors agreed upon as well as on Michael's use of his communication system, both prompted and independently.

Step 6: Evaluate Effectiveness and Generate Your Own Evidence

Building in More Predictability

The team met as planned three months later. Michael had made substantial progress in transitioning across homes, and the "change days" were no longer as difficult. He was also communicating more, mostly when prompted, but in the last few weeks, he had gone to get his iPad to tell his parents, at both homes, that he wanted to play outside. He was, with the support of the home-based paraprofessionals, consistently using the bathroom in each home, usually with reminders, but with almost no prompting. The team had done a task analysis (the process of breaking down a skill or set of skills into small, short, learnable components) and taught and reinforced each discrete step in the process, which proved to be a successful approach for Michael—and a tremendous relief for his parents. He seemed to enjoy his stays at the respite center, since the staff took the children on community outings and kept them engaged and active. The overnight stays also provided his parents with much-needed relief.

Unfortunately, there had been no decrease in Michael's bolting or throwing objects, or changes in his sleep patterns at either house. He would get through a few days with no events, but then his bolting would resurface. In fact, there was an increase in the intensity and frequency of his attempts, and he had pushed his mother and shoved a new babysitter at his father's house out of the door, making it all the way to the street in one instance. He was waking up more often at night and had figured out how to get out of his room. He remained safe, however, as alarms had been installed in both households. He had also developed a new behavior: banging his head on hard surfaces

when his attempts to bolt were blocked. Michael was able to participate in a few outings with the supervision of the paraprofessionals,
but only to safe, enclosed, locked areas or secure, gated playgrounds.
Otherwise, he would spend most of the time trying to find a way out.

At a follow-up appointment, Michael's neurologist reported
that the initial medication trial had not been successful. However,
he had experience with many other medications and was willing to
try a different one. Both parents agreed to this, but they knew that
medication alone would not solve all of their problems. Michael's
parents continued to feel exhausted and overwhelmed, even with
the addition of the paraprofessional and other supports. They both
felt that their lives were not manageable; safety was still a major
concern; and they also both felt that they weren't helping Michael
by keeping him home. Either they were confining him or chasing
after him. The only time they didn't need to be right next to him
was when the home-based team was there. One day he had even
bolted when they were playing in the fenced-in backyard.

Paul and Lauren called a team meeting and brought up the subject of a residential placement again. The school team agreed that
while some of their efforts had been successful, the most challenging of Michael's behaviors hadn't shown improvement, and a different, round-the-clock, more consistent approach would be more
effective, based on the data they had amassed so far, and would be
more likely to teach Michael to control his bolting, head-banging,
and throwing urges, and so that his family's health and well-being
could be preserved. Furthermore, if other medications were going
to be prescribed, Michael's parents felt they all needed more support
and Michael needed even more more consistent monitoring, which
could be achieved only in a residential program.

The school team agreed. Because the behavioral consultation
team was from a residential school for students with similar needs,
and several staff members already knew Michael, this seemed like
one school that should be considered.

Step 7: Redesign the Plan as Needed

Although Michael's parents had wanted a residential placement for some time and felt a sense of relief once it had been agreed upon by the entire team, they both had an unexpectedly difficult time adjusting emotionally. They felt guilty about not being able to provide for him at home, and they felt they had failed him. None of their friends' children, even the ones with disabilities, lived away from home. So why couldn't they manage their child? They also worried about his safety and wondered if the staff would take good care of him. They knew they were going to miss him and worried about his missing them.

Comprehensive Services Make a Major Impact

Upon entering the residential school, the family was assigned a social worker as well as a parent support group. Both were helpful in assuring them that their reactions were normal and that it takes all families time to adjust. They also got a visitation schedule, so they knew they could look forward to visiting the school often and that Michael would also be able to come home regularly. The staff reminded his parents how much Michael would continue to be part of their lives.

Michael's new school made a new plan, building on the one designed by the behavioral consulting team, and adding new components for carryover in his new residence. With this new level of consistency, Michael's behavior steadily improved over his first six months. He no longer engaged in head banging. He had not physically pushed anyone after the first few weeks. He was continuing to expand his communication. On his home visits after the first month, his behaviors also generalized, although not as consistently. School provided a home-based support person to assist during home visits and shortened them so he was more likely to be successful.

Michael's parents were pleased with his progress and gradually began to feel better—less guilty and certainly less exhausted. They came to the conclusion that they had made the right decision, and they were grateful for their team's support. Even more important, both his parents enjoyed their time with Michael more than they ever had and looked forward to seeing him. The teams from both his old and new schools and the family would meet after Michael had been in the program for a year to review his progress and determine if and when they could consider his returning to live at home and attend a full day, full year program at some point.

CHAPTER 12

JAKE: A 5-YEAR-OLD WHO HAS RESPONDED WELL TO FLOORTIME™

"We aren't the world's greatest experts on autism, but we are experts on knowing what works for our child. We just want to be able to continue."

—Jake's parents

Step 1: Gather Background Information

Jake's parents and school team had reached an impasse. His parents had seen him thrive since he was immediately enrolled in an intensive program that used a DIR®/Floortime™ model when he was diagnosed with PDD-NOS at age 2. His current program was using an eclectic approach that included a great deal of preacademic teaching. They also used a variety of approaches his parents disagreed with, such as teaching pretend play using video modeling, teaching social skills through social scripts, and using Discrete Trial Training for language and academic skills. Jake's parents had not enrolled him in the town's preschool program because of these disagreements, but now that he was about to enter Kindergarten, they were in a quandary. They wanted him to be with typical peers and neighborhood children, but they didn't want him in a classroom using approaches they didn't agree with. They did want his Floortime™ program to continue.

The school team and family agreed to have an independent evaluation performed by a mutually agreed upon educational consultant in order to identify his needs.

How It All Began

Jake is the third of three boys. His parents knew he was different from the other two, even during his first few weeks. He was much less active than his brothers, often stared off into space, and didn't try to catch their eyes. He was fussier and difficult to calm. Although he didn't get a diagnosis of autism until age 2, his parents started working with him, helping him learn to self-soothe, trying to get him to respond to them, from infancy.

Jake's mother was an occupational therapist, and both she and her husband, who was now in real estate, had extensive training and experience in Floortime.™ In fact, she had met her husband when they both worked in a Floortime™ program for several years before having children. They suspected Jake might end up with an autism spectrum diagnosis, and while she and her husband were very involved with all of their children, they worked especially hard with Jake from the start, knowing how important it was and also knowing how to work with him to get him more engaged and responsive.

When Jake was an infant, they worked on helping him reach a calm state and then sustain calmness when he became distressed. They found that reducing outside stimulation was especially helpful. When he was happy and relaxed, they gradually worked to entice him to look at them. They found he responded best to them when they engaged with him one parent at a time.

Their older children were eager to play with their new baby brother, and they showed his siblings how to hold and soothe Jake and then entice him to gradually turn his head and look at them. Their oldest, Marc, was especially skilled at this, which surprised his parents, since Marc was particularly boisterous and active. They found it very moving to watch their frequently out-of-control, noisy son quietly and gently lure Jake to look at him and then give his little brother a big smile in return. Marc was the first one in the family to get a flicker of a smile back from Jake!

Jake's parents first sought out a Floortime™-trained occupational therapist through Early Intervention. Although they knew a great deal about Floortime™, they felt outside input could also be helpful. With the OT assisting them, their Floortime™ program evolved and Jake became more and more engaged and responsive. He also learned to self-calm and regulate more easily and in a broader range of circumstances—at home, in the car, at his grandparents' homes, and even during whirlwind trips to the grocery store. He still got overwhelmed in crowded, noisy places, but he enjoyed watching his brothers roughhouse and would visually track their movements, giggle, and sometimes reach out to them.

Building a Home-Based Team

Over the next few years, Jake's family and their occupational therapist worked with him. The family added a speech therapist to his team, who, while not formally trained in DIR®/Floortime™, used play-based techniques to foster his language and social interactions. She also helped with oral motor stimulation, as his low muscle tone and oral motor planning difficulties were making feeding and articulation more difficult.

Jake made a great deal of progress. He began using word approximations, began saying single words and then short phrases, and he developed a strong social interest. His play skills were rapidly improving, and he began imitating and pretending, drawing on activities in his daily life. He imitated his father shaving and his mother cooking, and he would do so spontaneously and with the appropriate sound effects. He had a wonderful sense of humor and had begun to even tell jokes that weren't really funny, but made everyone laugh anyway. He initiated social games like hide-and-seek with his brothers at home and approached other children at the playground, although he could not yet keep up with their rapid chatter or follow along with their complicated play routines.

Jake's parents planned and facilitated playdates with a few neighborhood children, with whom he enjoyed crashing into pillows and building forts out of sofa cushions. His parents were very encouraged by his frequent smiles, laughter, and bids for more play.

Over the next few months, Jake acquired enough language to be able to have back-and-forth conversations lasting a few turns and had even longer conversations with playful vocalizations and nonlanguage sounds, like rhyming and exchanging nonsense words.

Jake's parents met with an educational consultant to talk about educational options. She met and observed Jake and listened closely to the family's story. She was impressed by their knowledge and dedication and by his progress. However, she wondered if he had made the progress because of the Floortime™ approach or because they had spent so much time with him. She also wondered if they used Floortime™ only because of their familiarity and professional experience with this kind of program and if other approaches might work just as well, or even better.

The consultant did not know much about Floortime™ but was interested enough to research and read about it on the DIR®/Floortime™ Foundation's website (www.icdl.com) and review some of the literature supporting this approach. She then met with the school team. They described their program and explained that they only used evidence-based approaches, including Discrete Trial Training, video modeling, and social scripts. They also talked about the many successes they had had with children with Jake's needs and were confident that they could provide an appropriate program for him, too.

Step 2: Identify the Problem

The problem was clear to all involved. The family had strong feelings about one approach and felt it was the right one for Jake, and the school felt equally strongly about the approaches they used. All of the approaches were supported by bodies of research demonstrating their efficacy. The educational consultant reviewed several summaries and some articles in their entirety related to each approach in an effort to make the most informed recommendations.

The school team felt, however, that Jake's academic skills would be neglected if they implemented a DIR®/Floortime™ program at school. They also had difficulty imagining a scenario in which they used one approach with one child and a different approach with the rest of the children.

Step 3: State the Hypothesis, Yours and Others'

After meeting Jake and his parents and hearing their story, the school team became more interested in learning about DIR®/Floortime™ although they continued to fully support their ABA program. The team leader had observed Jake the year before when the family had considered enrolling him in the town's preschool, and she could see how much progress he had made, especially when he played with his brothers and his parents. However, the school had worked hard to develop their program; they were proud of it, and the children in it were making progress toward their goals. The team had a great deal of data that clearly showed each student's trajectory in acquiring a variety of skills, primarily academic ones. It was working well, and they saw no reason to make major changes. They concluded that Jake would do as well as his classmates.

Jake's parents were not convinced. One of their major concerns was that a more structured teaching approach would actually interfere with his progress, especially in his natural, reciprocal interactions, and this was very important to them. They also felt that using video modeling for teaching pretend play would interfere with the more spontaneous, naturalistic ways he was acquiring pretend and imaginary play skills: through imitation and acting out real-life scenarios he observed at home daily. They didn't want him to learn to imitate pre-set scripted scenarios; rather, they wanted him to be able to play in a flexible way with peers, to interact, and to express his experiences, spontaneous thoughts, and feelings.

Step 4: Review Research

The educational consultant, school team, and home-based team discussed all of the approaches being used and cited some specific studies supporting each one. Furthermore, both school and family had clinical experience guiding their differing opinions. The school's behavioral consultant, a board-certified behavior analyst (BCBA), said she had been taught that only programs consistent with Applied Behavior Analysis (ABA) had enough evidence to be considered consistent with evidence-based practice (EBP), and she couldn't support use of DIR®/Floortime™. The educational consultant discussed evolving definitions and interpretations of EBP, and her perspective was that this orientation is based on a narrow interpretation of EBP. She also discussed several recent published research studies of DIR®/Floortime™, with positive outcomes. She then brought up the component of EBP that involves taking into account client preference as part of the treatment selection process as well as looking across a range of research data. This family was very committed to Floortime™, first as trained and experienced professionals, and then, as a result of seeing their son's ongoing progress. She thought it would be unlikely, even if Jake were enrolled in the ABA-based school program, that the family would embrace it, nor would they enthusiastically or consistently carry over the approaches being used, as it wasn't compatible with their beliefs or preferences.

Parent Involvement/Parent Demands

The team leader had many questions about this situation, asking if it meant that parents could dictate school practices and if the school had to provide any approach a family requested. The educational consultant assured her that family preference was but one of several components in EBP, and that research support and the child's history of progress were also part of the process for determining which approach to use. In her opinion, the school would have to shift its thinking. If the school team was committed to basing their programming on current definitions of EBP, this would result in getting training and developing expertise in or hiring consultants in more than one approach that also had evidence supporting its use for a particular child.

While the educational consultant said she couldn't determine if he would respond better or worse, or even at all, to the school's current programming, everyone who observed or assessed Jake agreed he had made quantifiable and qualifiable gains with DIR®/Floortime™. So for this child, the family had used evidence-based practice and subsequently had also generated practice-based evidence.

Step 5: Design the Treatment Plan

The school agreed to hire the family's Floortime™-trained occupational therapist to do training and consulting with the early childhood staff. They also agreed to employ a Floortime™-trained classroom assistant for Jake. They would measure and record his progress during the school year and then re-evaluate in the spring. They agreed not to use DTT teaching, include him in the social scripting group, or use video modeling, according to his parents' wishes.

The occupational therapist/Floortime™ therapist had recently evaluated Jake using the Functional Emotional Assessment Scale

(Greenspan & DeGangi, 2001), and the school team conducted separate evaluations. As a team they developed an IEP based on this combination of assessments, with goals highlighting social interaction, emotional regulation, symbolic play skills, and communication skills. Basic academics goals were also included, as this was part of the school's mandate, and Jake's parents agreed. The online DIR®/Floortime™ Goal Banks were helpful as templates for writing IEP goals that captured developmental achievements in the areas consistent with Floortime™.

Step 6: Evaluate Effectiveness and Generate Your Own Evidence

The school team enjoyed adding to their expertise by learning new approaches through the DIR®/Floortime™ training and consultation. The family was also pleased because the school was open to and willing to develop a truly individualized program for Jake.

It took Jake a few weeks to adjust to school and a more consistent routine, but soon it was clear that he was enjoying the program and was connecting well with his teachers and the rest of the staff. Over the next few months, he increasingly, with adult support, started engaging with his peers. At home the family continued working with him using DIR®/Floortime™ and meeting regularly with his Floortime™ therapist for continued support and consultation. The first quarterly IEP progress report indicated that Jake had already achieved many of the goals the team had laid out for the year.

AFTERWORD

By now maybe you have read this book cover to cover. Or perhaps you have skimmed it, or read a few chapters, or are skipping right to the conclusion. Whatever the case, we hope that you—the reader, teacher, therapist, parent, or student—recognize that planning and carrying out effective treatment for a child with an autism spectrum diagnosis is a complex, dynamic, and evolving process.

We have based this book and our process on current iterations of evidence-based practice, which incorporates individual children's characteristics and preferences, family beliefs, clinical judgment, and other difficult-to-quantify factors, and includes implementing treatments to work on goals that are important to the individual being treated, as well as evidence from various forms of research. We have drawn from and built on the work of others who have also elaborated what this practice means for autism treatment (Mesibov & Shea, 2011; Prizant, 2011).

Our goal is to help children with what they would choose to be helped with, in a way they would choose to be helped, if they were capable of making and communicating informed decisions. Children with autism often can't speak to these issues themselves in the usual way. So we adults, when speaking on their behalf, need to be especially attentive to their affective cues in evaluating if a particular treatment—if they could understand the range of possible treatments—would be consistent with their choice. Furthermore, would they want help with this problem if they could understand the impact of the problem and the possible solutions? One cannot ask children who are unable to communicate if they would like to engage in a process that might help them become better able to communicate. Yet one can prioritize this as a goal, knowing that the more these children can communicate, the better they will be at expressing their preferences and becoming more active, informed participants in their treatment process, as well as in their relationships and lives in general. Getting to know the individual children, their likes and dislikes, what is important to them, how they learn, and getting to know these same characteristics about their families and learning what they want help with are good places to start.

Families can readily speak to the issues of what they want their children to learn and what treatment approach(es) they want to use. Helping families understand the range of treatment options, the research supporting different treatments for the challenges they are working to resolve or skills they are trying to develop, and how they might benefit their children and/or whether they may cause new challenges, are important considerations in helping them make informed decisions. They need to know, as we do, that treatment choices are not straightforward within this field. These conversations must occur with an open mind, a listening ear, informed by clinical experience and knowledge of current clinical and research literature, and with awareness of one's own biases. We must be able to understand and work with family perspectives that may diverge from our own. And, if we are unable to work in concert with a family's preferences, because of lack of training or experience, philosophical differences, beliefs, or any other reasons, we are obligated to inform them.

As we have discussed throughout the book, evidence from research, as well as clinical experience and clinical judgment, are key components in guiding treatment. As we work with children and learn treatment approaches, we practitioners build our own internal database, then draw upon it when we make clinical judgments. It is important to listen carefully to these judgments and apply them in treatment planning, but it is equally important to continually question and revise our clinical judgment, as we add to our database through ongoing learning—from the children we work with, from their families, from our colleagues, from additional training, and from research findings.

Giving weight to clinical judgment is based on an assumption of clinical expertise. This involves ongoing learning, training, studying, and becoming increasingly proficient in what we are doing. This also involves working closely with and learning from colleagues with different kinds of expertise. Incorporating one's own clinical judgment into planning a child's treatment is a big responsibility and requires that we have a depth and breadth of training, knowledge, and experience. The process of gathering data as to one's effectiveness, of generating practice-based evidence, is also a process that enhances our own clinical skills and makes our clinical judgment increasingly valuable.

Being able to carry out a treatment plan based on an established model requires specific training. Some of the more comprehensive treatment models require very specific training and certification processes that can take years to attain (e.g., BCBA or DIR/Floortime™ certification), whereas other more specific and straightforward treatment approaches and methodologies do not (e.g., use of the Five-Point Scale or Social Stories). Every teacher, therapist, or program staff member cannot have advanced training and certification across multiple models. Consultation and supervision address this issue to some extent when they are available. Working directly with colleagues who have differing areas of expertise or virtually, through written and Internet resources are other ways to acquire a broader knowledge base.

Knowing how to evaluate research reliability and validity, or consulting with respected colleagues who know how to do this, is crucial to incorporating research evidence. Being able to determine which body of literature could have a bearing on a specific situation and how to interpret and use this information is as daunting as it is necessary. It is imperative to keep current, or work closely with those who do, with research findings from randomized controlled trials, and with promising developments in the field that have not yet been studied in randomized, controlled research but are based in clinically sound processes and that might, for other EBP reasons, be important to incorporate in your current treatment planning.

What if, after reading this book, you become inspired and energized about our complicated but very worthwhile field, and you charge back to school on Monday morning, ready to reexamine how you are working with Joey's daily tantrums. Then *wham!* Reality strikes, and you discover that (a) the funding for your classroom assistant has been cut and she will be gone in a week; (b) you have twins who will be starting in your class tomorrow, who don't have autism but have behavioral issues (but your class is the only one with behavioral consultation); (c) one parent is upset because you haven't started their child's toileting program; and (d) not only does Joey tantrum on his way into the school today as he has been doing even more frequently since a new behavioral plan was put in place, but he sits down in the hall and starts taking off his clothes. What about that reflective process you read about this past weekend? Could it possibly help you right now, in your classroom, with these children?

We hope that somehow it does, even in the most challenging circumstances. We hope it helps you to recognize that because you have to get Joey into the classroom one way or another, you might want to try using a different approach. Maybe you have a hunch (your clinical judgment) that trying to interact with him first in the hall, by bringing out a picture he made the day before when he was in a good mood, might help him shift gears, and it might make him want to follow you into the room—and forget about taking off his clothes. Later, you will make a plan to meet with his parents to get their perspective. You will ask the program consultant to do a literature search regarding any new studies to treat this behavioral pattern for children like Joey. You will ask the behavioral consultant to conduct a more comprehensive functional assessment. You will, based on this information, and together with his family and the consultant, develop a new plan, and then re-evaluate if this new plan is more successful.

And for those who have the luxury of more time for each child, more expert consultants, infrastructures of interdisciplinary support, more time to meet with families, and more time to reflect together, we hope this process will also be helpful to you.

Ultimately, we hope that with this book, we have contributed to supporting an understanding of a process that leads to progress in treatment development. In doing so we hope we are able to contribute to helping actual children and families beyond those we treat directly.

AUTISM TREATMENT
APPROACHES

The following interventions and approaches are by no means the only ones that are used to treat various symptoms and challenges common in children with autism spectrum disorders. They are, however, the ones that have been considered, described in some detail, or referred to in this book. Several have a strong research base and have been used with children with autism, and others have been used successfully for specific problems in children with autism and/or in other populations. A few approaches are emerging and are less well known, but in many cases, studies are underway to determine their efficacy. We think it is worth describing treatments in all of these categories and advise readers to further explore the approaches and look for reliable research studies that support the approaches that interest them.

Many books and articles have been written about all of these approaches. Here you will find very brief explanations and summaries that are meant to inform and to guide further investigation.

Applied Behavior Analysis (ABA)

In the simplest terms, ABA is a scientifically based and comprehensive approach based on the principles of behavioral learning theory, pioneered by B. F. Skinner, which is used to modify and improve socially significant behaviors.

ABA focuses on observable behaviors, their function, and their relationship to the environment. It is often considered a first-line approach to treating autism and has a large body of research support. Instruction occurs by breaking down skills into their smallest, simplest components and then building on each component to teach increasingly complex skill sets. Learning occurs by reinforcing (rewarding) the proper execution of each component, skill, or skill set.

Cognitive-Behavioral Therapy (CBT)

Based on both cognitive and behavioral research, CBT is an approach to changing behaviors and thought processes, especially those that are a result of dysfunctional emotions and thought patterns. It often consists of a systematic set of procedures, guided by a trained therapist, that one can follow to achieve specific goals decided on by the individual and/or family. It is used to treat a variety of problems that can interfere with academic and social functioning, including stress-related and anxiety disorders, mood disorders, substance abuse and eating disorders, and other behaviors related to health and relationships. CBT can be used in one-on-one and group therapeutic settings.

This approach is also used in working with children with high-functioning autism and Asperger's disorder who have the attention, verbal communication skills, and cognitive ability to follow through on instructions and homework, which is often given as part of a CBT program.

Collaborative Problem Solving (CPS)

Collaborative Problem Solving (CPS) is a model, first described in the book *The Explosive Child*, by Ross Greene, PhD (1998), and in subsequent revisions and then expanded upon in *Treating Explosive Kids*, by Ross Greene and Stuart Ablon (2006) for treating challenging behaviors in children and adolescents. It is based on the theory that children's inappropriate and maladaptive behaviors are a result of developmental delays and "lagging skills" in such areas as flexibility, tolerance for frustration, and considering alternative solutions.

The CPS model describes three options for problem solving that parents typically use with children: Plan A, unilateral decision making; Plan B, drop the problem entirely; and Plan C, the collaborative approach. Like CBT, using CPS requires that the individual have adequate verbal and cognitive skills to be able to discuss specific challenges and access the solutions. Those with high-functioning autism and Asperger's syndrome are most likely to benefit from this approach to conflict resolution, both at school and at home.

DIR®/Floortime™

DIR®/Floortime™ is a Developmental–Individual Difference–Relationship-based model for assessing and developing an intervention program for children with autism spectrum disorders, based on their unique strengths and challenges. The major focus of this approach, created by Stanley L. Greenspan, MD, and Serena Weider, PhD, is helping children develop healthy emotional, social, and intellectual capacities, rather than beginning with teaching specific skills.

The model's central principle is the consideration of the child's natural emotions and interests and using and building upon them to stimulate increasingly higher levels of social, emotional, and intellectual capacities. DIR®/Floortime™ is often considered a playful, high-affect intervention that includes physical activity, toy play, problem solving, and social reciprocity. It can include center-based and home-based programming and both individual and small peer-group formats.

Early Start Denver Model (ESDM)

This is an intensive intervention approach for working with very young children with autism spectrum disorders that emphasizes spontaneous communication and social interaction. Through priming, scaffolding, rewarding, and increasing children's initiations and supporting parents and other providers in interpreting children's cues and extending those interactions, social learning opportunities are increased. The ESDM shares features with many models, such as DIR/Floortime™, SCERTS™, and RDI, especially in its emphasis on child positive affect. It also stresses data collection and evaluation and follows the principles of operant learning, using the ABA tools of prompting, fading, shaping, and chaining.

Functional Behavioral Assessment (FBA)

This is a systematic process for collecting information about the purposes (functions) of an individual's problem behaviors. An FBA incorporates both direct (observation) and indirect (interviewing key people; examining records) methods and results in a hypothesis—or several—about the causes of the behavior and the creation of an individualized behavior intervention plan designed to decrease problem behaviors and increase appropriate ones. A variety of useful recording forms and interview scripts are available in books, and some can be downloaded free of charge from numerous websites.

Picture Exchange Communication System (PECS)

PECS is a form of augmentative and assistive communication developed by Andy Bondy, PhD, and Carol Frost, CC-SLP, for students with autism and other disabilities for whom spoken language is inadequate. It is taught in phases, beginning with teaching students to present pictures of desired objects (toys, food, activities) to communication partners in exchange for those objects. Subsequent phases teach children how to use pictures in more socially complex ways, eventually combining pictures to make whole sentences and ask and answer questions. The goal is to promote functional, social, and spontaneous communication. PECS is often taught and used successfully with very young children, in preschool programs, and even prior to school placement. It is compatible with and enhances other treatment approaches; it requires some training but a limited investment in complex equipment or materials; and it is an effective means for getting students with various cognitive and social profiles communicating and interacting with each other. PECS can be used at school, at home, and in the community and, according to studies, it does not inhibit the development of spoken language and may promote speech acquisition.

Pivotal Response Training (PRT)

This technique is based on the principles of Applied Behavior Analysis (ABA) and focuses on motivation and responsivity as the key features of intervention. Usually conducted in more naturalistic settings, PRT was originally designed to identify and teach so-called pivotal behaviors, which, when learned, were thought to improve functioning across a wide range of other nontargeted but socially relevant behaviors, such as response generalization, spontaneity, self-management, and self-initiation. It is more child-directed than Discrete Trial Training (DTT) and prioritizes language, play, and social behaviors.

Positive Behavioral Supports (PBS)

This term is used broadly and in several ways. In the most general and commonly accepted terms, PBS is an applied set of principles that utilize educational and systems change methodology to minimize problem behaviors and allow people with disabilities greater access to community resources and educational, social, and recreational opportunities. It is not a rigid curriculum, but rather, a way of applying principles to teach adaptive behaviors and promoting more independent functioning. PBS draws from three major sources: Applied Behavior Analysis (ABA), the normalization and inclusion movement for people with disabilities, and person-centered values. PBS has been the subject of numerous research studies over the past 20 years, many of which have been published in professional publications and peer-reviewed journals. *The Journal of Positive Behavioral Interventions* is one journal devoted entirely to the publication of such studies.

Relationship Development Intervention (RDI)

Created by Steven E. Guttstein, PhD, RDI is a comprehensive, parent-centered model and curriculum for addressing the core deficits of autism by building dynamic intelligence, or the ability to respond in novel situations. It is composed of six levels and 24 stages that provide a path for children to learn skills for building friendships, empathy, and social reciprocity. It includes such objectives as flexible thinking, attention shifting, reflection, emotional regulation, improvisation, creativity, and problem solving.

Replays®

Replays® is a play-based approach developed to help children with behavioral difficulties that are caused by rapid, intense, often negative emotional responding. Occurrences such as loud and unexpected noises (thunder, fire alarms), broken toys, haircuts, toothbrushing, changes in schedule, taking medicine, and other common events can create extreme upsets in children with autism spectrum and related disorders. By playing through such events with a trusted adult, with the use of symbolic toys (dolls, action figures) or actual role playing, and by incorporating exaggerated affect, silly voices, and other "signals of play," the child begins to master the challenging situation and become desensitized, ultimately reducing its impact.

This approach has only case study support although it is based on a combination of approaches with substantial research backing.

SCERTS™ Model

The acronym SCERTS stands for Social Communication–Emotional Regulation and Transactional Support and focuses on developing and improving functional skills in everyday activities across settings for children with developmental ages of 8 months through 10 years. Developed by Barry M. Prizant, PhD; Amy M. Wetherby, PhD; Emily Rubin, MS; and Amy C. Laurent, OTR-L, this comprehensive, multidisciplinary framework addresses the core challenges faced by children with autism and related disabilities. It provides a continuum of semistructured to more natural social activities that are most conducive to addressing educational priorities, and emphasizes those that are developmentally appropriate and responsive to family priorities. The SCERTS™ process is logical and sequential, moving from assessment to educational programming.

Sensory Integration Therapy/Sensory Diets

Sensory Integration is a therapeutic approach that enhances the brain's ability to process sensory information. It incorporates the use of a variety of sensory materials and physical input in order to improve a child's ability to attend and focus, regulate moods and activity, and tolerate environmental change. SI therapy often helps reduce negative reactions to stimuli, such as noise (fire alarms, loud voices), crowded spaces (school assemblies, the cafeteria), textures of fabrics, and food and play materials (clothing labels, mushy or chewy foods, Play-Doh). A sensory diet refers to the systematic scheduling and use of these sensory materials and activities at key times throughout a student's day in order to improve functioning in one or more of these areas.

Social Stories™

Social Stories™ is a technique created by Carol Gray in 1991 that describes a situation, skill, or concept according to 10 specific characteristics. Often used to address behavioral difficulties in the classroom, Social Stories™ are not meant necessarily to change a child's behavior, but rather, to improve his or her understanding of the events and expectations in a given situation that may be confusing or challenging, This, in turn, may lead to the child's improved ability to manage the situation.

References

Ablon, J. S., Levy, R., & Katzenstein, T. (2006). Beyond brand names of psychotherapy: Identifying empirically supported change processes. *Psychotherapy: Theory, Research, Practice, Training, 43*(2), 216–231.

Ahern, L., & Rosenthal, E. (2010). *Torture not treatment: Electric shock and long-term restraint in the United States on children and adults with disabilities at the Judge Rotenberg Center.* Washington, DC: Mental Disability Rights International.

Amado, A., & McBride, M. (2001). *Person-centered planning facilitators: A compendium of ideas.* Minneapolis: University of Minnesota, Institute on Community Integration.

American Psychiatric Association. (2000). *Diagnostic and statistical manual of mental disorders* (4th ed., rev., DSM-IV). Washington, DC: Author.

American Psychological Association, Division 12, Society of Clinical Psychology. (1995). Retrieved from: www.apa.org/divisions /div12/cppi.html

American Psychological Association, APA Presidential Task Force on Evidence-Based Practice. (2006). Evidence-based practice in psychology. *American Psychologist, 61,* 271–285.

American Speech-Language-Hearing Association Executive Board. (2004). *Evidence-based practice in communication disorders: An introduction* [Technical report]. Retrieved from www.asha.org /policy

Attwood, T. (2006). *The complete guide to Asperger's syndrome.* London: Jessica Kingsley.

Bachmeyer, M. H., Piazza, C. C., Fredrick, L. D., Reed, G. K., Rivas, K. D., & Kadey, H. J. (2009). Functional analysis and treatment of multiply controlled inappropriate mealtime behavior. *Journal of Applied Behavior Analysis, 42*(3), 641–658.

Bany-Winters, L. (1997). On stage: *Theatre games and activities for kids.* Chicago: Chicago Review Press.

Baron-Cohen, S., & Wheelwright, S. (2004). The Empathy Quotient (EQ): An investigation of adults with Asperger syndrome or high functioning autism, and normal sex differences. *Journal of Autism and Developmental Disorders, 34,* 163–175.

Bauminger, N., & Kasari, C. (2003). Loneliness and friendship in high-functioning children with autism. *Child Development, 71*(2), 447–456.

Bellini, S., & Akullian, J. (2007). A meta-analysis of video modeling and video self-modeling interventions for children and adolescents with autism spectrum disorders. *Exceptional Children, 73*(3), 264–287.

Birmaher, B., Ehmann, M., Axelson, D., Goldstein, B., Monk, K., Kalas, C., . . . Brent, D. (2009). Schedule for affective disorders and schizophrenia for school-age children (K-SADS-PL) — for the assessment of preschool children: A preliminary psychometric study. *Journal of Psychiatric Research, 43*(7), 680–686.

Bondy, A., & Frost, L. (2001). *A picture's worth: PECS and other visual communication strategies in autism.* Bethesda, MD: Woodbine.

Bromfield, R. (2011). *Embracing Asperger's: A primer for parents and professionals.* London: Jessica Kingsley.

Charlop, M. H., Schreibman, L., & Thibodeau, M. G. (1985). Increasing spontaneous verbal responding in autistic children using a time delay procedure. *Journal of Applied Behavior Analysis*, *18*(2), 155–166.

Cochrane, A. (1972). *Effectiveness and efficiency: Random reflections on health services.* London: Nuffield Provincial Hospitals Trust.

Curtis, L., & Patel, K. (2008). Nutritional and environmental approaches to preventing and treating autism and Attention Deficit Hyperactivity Disorder (ADHD): A review. *Journal of Alternative and Complementary Medicine*, *14*(1), 79–85.

Dawson, G., Rogers, S., Munson, J., Winter, J., Greenson, J., Donaldson, A., & Varely, J. (2010). Randomized, controlled trial of an intervention for toddlers with autism: The Early Start Denver Model, *Pediatrics*, *125*(1), e17–23.

Downey, G., & Coyne, J. (1990). Children of depressed parents: An integrative review. *Psychological Bulletin*, *108*(1), 50–76.

Duncan, B. L., Miller, S. D., & Sparks, J. A. (2004). *The heroic client: A revolutionary way to improve effectiveness* (Revised). San Francisco: Jossey-Bass.

Eggers, C., Bunk, D., & Krause, D. (2000). Schizophrenia with onset before the age of eleven: Clinical characteristics of onset and course. *Journal of autism and developmental disorders*, *30*(1), 29–38.

Elder, J., & Thomas, M. (2005). *Different like me: My book of autism heroes.* London: Jessica Kingsley.

Frank, A. R., Wacker, D. P., Berg, W. K., & McMahon, C. M. (1985). Teaching selected microcomputer skills to retarded students via picture prompts. *Journal of Applied Behavior Analysis*, *18*, 179–185.

Gagnon, E., & Smith Myles, B. (1999). *This is Asperger syndrome.* Overland Park, KS: Asperger Publishing.

Garcia Winner, M. (2008). *Superflex . . . A superhero social thinking curriculum.* San Jose, CA: Think Social/Social Thinking.

Gillis, J. M., Natof, T. H., Lockshin, S. B., & Romanczyk, R. G. (2009). Fear of routine physical exams in children with autism spectrum disorders. *Focus on Autism & Other Developmental Disabilities, 24*, 156–168.

Greene, R. (1998). *The explosive child: A new approach for understanding and parenting easily frustrated, chronically inflexible children*. New York: Harper.

Greene, R., & Ablon, J. S. (2006). *Treating explosive kids: The collaborative problem-solving approach*. New York: Guilford Press.

Greenspan, S. I., & DeGangi, G. (2001). Research on the FEAS: Test development, reliability, and validity studies. In S. Greenspan, G. DeGangi, & S. Wieder (Eds.), *The Functional Emotional Assessment Scale (FEAS) for infancy and early childhood: Clinical and research applications* (pp. 167–247). Bethesda, MD: Interdisciplinary Council on Developmental and Learning Disorders (ICDL).

Greenspan, S., & Wieder, S. (2006). *Engaging autism: Using the Floortime approach to help children relate, communicate and think*. New York: de Capo Press.

Gutstein, S., & Sheely, R. (2002). *Relationship development intervention with young children: Social and emotional activities for Asperger syndrome, autism, PDD, and NLD*. London: Jessica Kingsley.

Hadwin, J., Howlin, P., & Baron-Cohen, S. (2008). *Teaching children with autism to mindread: A handbook. Hoboken*, NJ: Wiley.

Jerome, J., Frantino, E. P., & Sturmey, P. (2007). The effects of errorless learning and backward chaining on the acquisition of Internet skills in adults with developmental disabilities. *Journal of Applied Behavioral Analysis, 40*(1), 185–189.

Kasari, C., Freeman, S., & Paparella, T. (2006). Joint attention and symbolic play in young children with autism: A randomized controlled intervention study. *Journal of Child Psychology and Psychiatry, 48*(5), 523.

Kaufman, J., Birmaher, B., Brent, D., Rao, U., Flynn, C., Moreci, P., . . . Ryan, N. (1997). Schedule for affective disorders and schizophrenia for school-age children—Present and lifetime version (K-SADS-PL): Initial reliability and validity data. *Journal of the American Academy of Child and Adolescent Psychiatry, 36*(7), 980–988.

Koegel, L. K. (1995). Communication and language intervention. In R. L. Koegel & L. K. Koegel (Eds.), *Teaching children with autism: Strategies for initiating positive interactions and improving learning opportunities* (pp. 17–32). Baltimore: Brookes.

Koegel, R., Vernon, T. W., & Koegel, L. K. (2009). Improving social initiations in young children with autism using reinforcers with embedded social interactions. *Journal of Autism and Developmental Disorders, 39*(9), 1240–1251.

Kormann, R. J., & Petronko, M. R. (2003). Crisis and revolution in developmental disabilities: The dilemma of community-based services. *The Behavior Analyst Today, 3*(4), 434–443.

Landa, R. J., Holman, K. C., O'Neill, A. H., & Stuart, E. A. (2011). Intervention targeting development of socially synchronous engagement in toddlers with autism spectrum disorder: A randomized controlled trial. *Journal of Child Psychology and Psychiatry, 52*(1), 13–21.

Lerner, M. D., Mikami, A. Y., & Levine, K. (2010). Socio-dramatic affective-relational intervention for adolescents with Asperger syndrome and high-functioning autism: Pilot study. *Autism, 15*(1), 21–42,

Levine, K., & Chedd, N. (2007). *Replays: Using play to enhance emotional and behavioral development for children with autism spectrum disorders.* London: Jessica Kingsley.

Levine, K., Chedd, N., & Bauch, D. (2009). The social-affective diet. *Autism Spectrum Quarterly*, Fall.

Magnuson, K., & Constantino, J. (2011). Characterization of depression in children with autism spectrum disorders. *Journal of Developmental & Behavioral Pediatrics, 32*(4), 332–340.

Mattila, M., Hurtig, T., Haapsamo, H., Jussila, K., Kuusikko-Gauffin, S., Kielinen, M., . . . Moilanen, I. (2009). Comorbid psychiatric disorders associated with Asperger syndrome/high-functioning autism: A community- and clinic-based study. *Journal of Autism and Developmental Disorders, 40*(9), 1080–1093.

McReynolds, P. (1997). *Lightner Witmer: His life and times.* Washington, DC: American Psychological Association.

Mesibov, G.B., & Shea, V. (2011). Evidence-based practices and autism. *Autism, 15*(1), 114–133.

Meyer, D. (2007). *Sibshops: Workshops for siblings of children with special needs.* Baltimore: Brookes.

Millar, D., Light, J., & Schlosser, R. (2006). The impact of augmentative and alternative communication intervention on the speech production of individuals with developmental disabilities: A research review. *Journal of Speech, Language, and Hearing Research, 49*, 248–264.

Mostert, M., & Kavale, K. (2001). Evaluation of research for usable knowledge in behavioral disorders: Ignoring the irrelevant, considering the germane. *Behavioral Disorders, 27*(1), 53–68.

National Research Committee on Educational Interventions for Children with Autism, National Research Council. (2001). *Educating children with autism.* Washington, DC: National Academy of Sciences.

National Research Council. (2001). *Educating children with autism.* Washington, DC: The National Academies Press.

Odum, S.L., Brian, B.A., Hall, L.J. & Hume, K. (2010) Evaluation of comprehensive Treatment models for individuals with autism spectrum disorders.

Parker-Pope, T. (2009, December 22). Raising I.Q. in toddlers with autism. *The New York Times*. Retrieved from: http://well.blogs.nytimes.com/2009/12/22/iq-boost-for-toddlers-with-autism/

Prizant, B. (2011). The use and misuse of evidence-based practice implications for persons with ASD. *Autism Spectrum Quarterly*, 15, 43–49.

Prizant, B., & Wetherby, A. (1998). Understanding the continuum of discrete-trial traditional behavioral to social-pragmatic developmental approaches in communication enhancement for young children with autism/PDD. *Seminars in Speech Language*, *19*(4), 329–352.

Prizant, B., Wetherby, A., Rubin, E., Laurent, A., & Rydell, P. (2006). *The SCERTS Model: A comprehensive educational approach for children with autism spectrum disorders*. Baltimore: Brookes.

Reichow, B., Doehring, P., Cicchetti, D.V. & Volkmar, F. R. (Eds.) (2011) Evidence-based practices and treatment for Children with autism, New York: Springer.

Rogers, S. (1998). Empirically supported comprehensive treatments for young children with autism. *Journal of Clinical Child Psychology*, *27*(2), 168–179.

Rogers, S., & Dawson, G. (2009). *Early Start Denver Model for young children with autism*. New York: Guilford Press.

Rogers, S., & Vismara, L. (2008). Evidence-based comprehensive treatments for early autism. *Journal of Child & Adolescent Psychology*, *37*(1), 8–38.

Rutter, M. (1990). Functional emotional assessment scale. *Developmental Psychology*, *26*(1), 60–67.

Ryburn, B., Anderson, V., & Wales, R. (2009). Asperger syndrome: How does it relate to non-verbal learning disability? *Journal of Neuropsychology*, *3*(1), 107–123.

Sackett, D., Rosenberg, W., Gray, J., Haynes, R., & Richardson, W. (1996). Evidence-based medicine: What it is and what it isn't. *British Medical Journal*, *312*(3), 71–72.

Schlosser, R., Koul, R., & Costello, J. (2007). Asking well-built questions for evidence-based practice in augmentative and alternative communication. *Journal of Communication Disorders, 40*(3), 225–238.

Schneider, C. (2007). *Acting antics: A theatrical approach to teaching social understanding to kids and teens with Asperger syndrome.* London: Jessica Kingsley.

Shabani, D., & Fisher, W. (2006). Stimulus fading in differential reinforcement for the treatment of needle phobia in a youth with autism. *Journal of Applied Behavioral Analysis, 39*(4), 449–452.

Simonoff, E., Pickles, A., Charman, T., Chandler, S., Loucas, T., & Baird, G. (2008). Psychiatric disorders in children with autism spectrum disorders: Prevalence, comorbidity, and associated factors in a population-derived sample. *Journal of the American Academy of Child and Adolescent Psychiatry, 47*(8), 921–929.

Sloper, T., & Beresford, B. (2006). Families with disabled children: Social and economic needs are high but remain largely unmet. *British Medical Journal, 333*(7575), 928–929.

Sturmey, P. (2005). Secretin is a robustly ineffective treatment for autism: A review of 15 double-blind randomized controlled trials. *Research in Developmental Disabilities, 26*, 87–97.

Sulzer-Azaroff, B., Hoffman, A. O., Horton, C. B., Bondy, A., & Frost, L. (2009). The picture exchange communication system (PECS): What do the data say? *Focus on Autism and Other Developmental Disabilities, 24*(2), 89–103.

Volkert, V. M., & Vaz, P. C. (2010). Recent studies on feeding problems in children with autism. *Journal of Applied Behavioral Analysis, 43*(1), 155–159.

Wagner, A. (2002). *What to do when your child has obsessive-compulsive disorder: Strategies and solutions.* Apex, NC: Lighthouse.

Wagner, A. (2005). *Worried no more: Help and hope for anxious children* (2nd ed.). Apex, NC: Lighthouse.

Ward, S., Sylva, J., & Gresham, F. M. (2010). School-based predictors of early adolescent depression. *School Mental Health, 2*(3), 125–131.

Ward, S., Sylva, J., & Gresham, F. M. (2012). School-based predictors of early adolescent depression. *School Mental Health, 2*(3), 125–130.

Werner, E., & Dawson, G. (2005). Validation of the phenomenon of autistic regression using home videotapes. *Archives of General Psychiatry, 62*(8), 889–895.

Whitehouse, A., Durkin, K., Jaquet, E., & Ziatas, K. (2009). Friendship, loneliness and depression in adolescents with Asperger's syndrome. *Journal of Adolescence, 32*(2), 309–322.

Wilczynski, S., Green, G., Ricciardi, J., Boyd, B., Hume, A., Ladd, M., . . . Rue, H. (2009). *National Standards Report: The National Standards Project—Addressing the need for evidence-based practice guidelines for autism spectrum disorders.* Randolph, MA: National Autism Center.

Wine, A. (2005). *What it is to be me!: An Asperger kid book.* Fairdale, KY: Fairdale Publishing.

Winner, M. G. (2008) . A *politically incorrect look at evidence-based practices and teaching social skills.* San Jose, CA: Think Social Publishing.

Wood, J. J., Drahota, A., Sze, K., Har, K., Chiu, A., & Langer, D. A. (2009). Cognitive behavioral therapy for anxiety in children with autism spectrum disorders: A randomized, controlled trial. *Journal of Child Psychology and Psychiatry, 50,* 224–234.

Wood, J., Drahota, A., Sze, K., Van Dyke, M., Decker, K., Fujii, C., . . . Spiker, M. (2009). Effects of cognitive behavioral therapy on parent-reported autism symptoms in school-age children with high-functioning autism. *Journal of Autism and Developmental Disorders, 39*(11), 1608–1612.

Zwaigenbaum, L., Bryson, S., Rogers, T., Roberts, W., Brian, J., & Szatmari, P. (2005). Behavioral manifestations of autism in the first year of life. *International Journal of Developmental Neuroscience*, 23(2-3), 143–152.

AUTHOR INDEX

Subject Index